"Jim Miller's book puts into simple, interesting, and enjoyable reading proven techniques on how you can create a 'winning' culture for employees, customers, and organizations. The 'Coach's Checklist' at the end of each chapter should be read by everyone in business."

—Bruce Nelson, president and CEO of BT Office Products USA

"When it comes to guiding companies and individuals to new heights, Jim Miller 'wrote the book,' figuratively speaking. Now he has done it, literally!"

—The Hon. Tom Vandergriff, former U.S. congressman of the Twenty-sixth District (Texas)

"How to reward employees and still make a profit; how to please clients without giving away the store; how to create a joyful, dedicated workforce and repeat customers; Jim Miller shows you how in *The Corporate Coach*. He has made me even more committed to his philosophy while giving me additional ideas on how to continue to improve in these areas."

—Sheila Cluff, president of The Oaks at Ojai

"Winning in business in the nineties takes more than a sound strategy and an ability to squeeze out costs. It takes superior execution on the part of knowledgeable, customer-focused employees working as a team. Jim Miller takes us step-by-step down a path that leads to the creation of a top-tier customer-service organization. He's given managers the perfect game plan for improving their companies' customer focus and employee morale."

—George R. Trumbull, president of Connecticut General Life Insurance Company

P9-CES-411

## *Sports Figure Endorsements*

"Jim Miller has authored the premier motivation book for any company. This should be required reading in the business world. For that matter, I know many professional sports franchises that should incorporate this logic."

—Jim W. Nantz III, commentator for CBS Sports

"Finally a book about simply, usable, and common-sense ideas that all coaches should follow. It is amazing to me how Jim Miller uses the same teamwork techniques that are a common thread in all successful athletic teams. What a magnificent gift for all 'coaches.'"

—Rich Donnelly, coach for the Pittsburgh Pirates

"If staying close to your customers is crucial to your business performance, then *The Corporate Coach* should be required reading. The message is well organized, well written, and more important, well practiced by the highly successful Miller teams."

—Michael H. Stone, former president of the Texas Rangers

## Executive Endorsements

"Jim Miller's message is a particularly powerful one in these competitive times. I wholeheartedly endorse the fundamentals of teamwork and customer service as essential ingredients for business success."

—William R. Howell, Chairman of the Board and CEO of the J.C. Penney Company, Inc.

"No game plan is effective without a leader who has the vision to build a *team*. Jim Miller has hit the bull's-eye in relating the importance of a team through his years of practical experience. It is enjoyable reading and an excellent tool for learning."

—Howard Putnam, former CEO of Braniff and Southwest Airlines

*"The Corporate Coach* is a practical guide to exceptional service through teamwork. This powerful playbook is full of inspiring and immediately implementable ideas that work!"

—Donald D. Belcher, group vice-president of Avery Dennison

"Jim Miller has condensed his experiences in building his service business into a highly readable book. It's so on target for CEOs and entrepreneurs that I'm voting it on my must read *today* list. The book reads like Jim talks and thinks and if you want to skip any of your mistakes and just do the right things, Jim shows you how."

—Joseph R. Mancuso, president of the Center for Entrepreneurial Management, Inc.

*"The Corporate Coach* puts into sharp focus that which we may know as managers, but many times, ignore in practice. It is an excellent checklist for success."

—Bob Doucette, chairman of Milwaukee Insurance Company

*"The Corporate Coach* is filled with 'common sense' that unfortunately is not taught in our system of formal education. This book should be required reading in every business school."

—Joseph R. Musolino, vice-chairman of NationsBank of Texas

"Fascinating! Jim Miller definitely has a knack for bringing some conceptual ideas to an easily readable and understandable format. This book will definitely be recommended reading for all current and future Steelcase dealers."

—Robert Pew, president of S/C Operations, Steelcase, Inc.

"Finally, a book that proves customers buy integrity. Practice what 'Coach' Jim Miller preaches and your company will be a winner. And the company 'team' will enjoy every inning and every quarter of the game."

—John J. Stollenwerk, president of the Allen Edmonds Shoe Corporation

"Jim Miller's enthusiasm is an inspiration. He makes business more fun and more profitable."

—Carl Sewell, author of *Customers for Life*

# The
# Corporate
# Coach

# JAMES B. MILLER

# The
# Corporate
# Coach

## WITH PAUL B. BROWN
## FOREWORD BY RON ZEMKE

**HarperBusiness**
*A Division of HarperCollinsPublishers*

This book was originally published in 1993 by St. Martin's Press. It is here reprinted by arrangement with St. Martin's Press.

HarperCollins books may be purchased for educational, business, or sales promotional use. For information please write: Special Markets Department, HarperCollins Publishers, Inc., 10 East 53rd Street, New York, NY 10022.

First HarperBusiness edition published 1994.

*Designed by Judith Christensen*

Library of Congress Cataloging-in-Publication Data

Miller, James B. (James Bernard), 1930–
    The corporate coach / James B. Miller with Paul B. Brown ; foreword by Ron Zemke.
  —1st HarperBusiness ed.
     p.  cm.
    Originally published : New York : St. Martin's Press, 1993.
    Includes index.
    ISBN 0-88730-685-3
    1. Psychology, Industrial.  2. Employee motivation.  3. Interpersonal relations.
  4. Work groups.  5. Customer service.
I. Brown, Paul B.  II. Title
[HF5548.8.M4924 1994]
158.7—dc20                                        93-47060

94 95 96 97 98 RRD 10 9 8 7 6 5 4 3 2 1

IN MEMORY OF MY PARENTS, BERNARD AND AURELIA MILLER, WHOSE GUIDANCE, LOVE, SUPPORT, AND EXAMPLE WERE AN INSPIRATION TO ME DURING THE EARLY YEARS OF ENTREPRENEURSHIP.

FOR MY FAMILY—MY WIFE, JOAN; SONS, MIKE AND GREG; AND DAUGHTER, KATHY—FOR THEIR SUPPORT AND COMMITMENT TO HELP OUR BUSINESS GROW AND SUCCEED.

FOR ALL MY TEAM PLAYERS AT ALL OUR COMPANIES, MILLER BUSINESS SYSTEMS, BUSINESS INTERIORS, AND AMERICAN DISCOUNT OFFICE FURNITURE.

# CONTENTS

# ACKNOWLEDGMENTS

For the encouragement and support of this book, I will be forever grateful to:

*Joan,* my wife, for the encouragement and support to buy a nearly bankrupt business and to work countless hours to help turn that venture into the success all six hundred employees currently enjoy. Also for her persistence in prodding me to write this book in order to share my ideas with people in the business world.

Our son *Michael,* daughter *Kathy,* and son *Greg,* for their love and patience during the early years of building the business and for the *terrific* job each one currently is doing in leadership positions in our various businesses.

*John Ward,* our family business consultant, who has offered sage advice through the years and who has played a major role in our three children's success in our business.

*Ron Zemke,* not only for featuring our firm in his publication *The Service Edge,* but also for encouraging me to write this book and share my philosophy with corporate America.

*Joe Mancuso,* of the Center for Entrepreneurial Management, for his suggestions over the years and for the opportunity to discuss and share my ideas with his CEO clubs.

*Debbie Kaplan,* for her legal guidance throughout this project.

*Jane and Bob Handly,* from Life Plus, who have successfully published five books and who were my mentors for this publication.

*Jeff Herman,* my literary agent, whose positive attitude and hard work have helped make this book a reality.

*George Witte,* my editor at St. Martin's Press, for his faith and confidence that this book can be of assistance to large and small corporations, as well as aspiring entrepreneurs.

*Rick Frishman, David Hahn,* and all the employees of Planned Television Arts, Ltd., for their enthusiasm and advice regarding the marketing of this publication. Their encouragement has been most helpful.

*Sharon Wells* and *Kay Smith,* my secretaries, for their continuing feedback, critiques, and suggestions for refinements to the book, as well as their willingness to retype manuscript revisions throughout the editing process.

*Mike Miller* and *Kathryn Gressett* of Miller Business Systems, and *John Sample* of Business Interiors, for their advice on improvements to this book.

*Beth Simon,* for her creative suggestions on the book jacket design.

*Harold Shaw,* former purchasing agent in Arlington, Texas, who gave me one of my first orders on June 13, 1967, and to *Ben Palmer,* retired LTV procurement manager, whose firm placed the first contract order with us in 1967. Both of these gentlemen gave me moral support when things looked bleak in the early years.

*All the members of the National Office Products Association* for their help and guidance during the past twenty-five years.

*Jane Wood,* who offered helpful personal advice and encouragement.

*Dianna Booher,* for her assistance early in this project and particularly for her work on the original proposal for the publisher.

. . . and to *Paul B. Brown* for the countless hours reviewing the audio tapes, for the interviews, and for his patience, which were necessary for him to help complete this manuscript.

Twenty-five years ago, when Jim and Joan Miller pulled up stakes, moved from Wisconsin to Texas, bought a near-bankrupt office-products store, and thereby began what has become Miller Business Systems and Business Interiors ($150 million in 1992 sales), they had two important things going for them. First, they had almost no money; second, they knew next to nothing about running a retail office-products business. Had they had either, there would very likely be no Miller Business Systems today.

Lacking the dollars and sense to do things the "right" way—the way everyone else did things in the industry—their recourse was to work like heck and throw themselves on the mercy of their employees and customers. *Not* knowing the office-products business meant that the Millers had to listen closely and carefully to their customers. When a customer said "I want," the Millers had to "go get"—they had to focus on responsiveness, not slick salesmanship, to land an order. When a customer complained, or when the Millers got something wrong, they apologized, atoned for the error, and figured out how to keep from making that mistake again. They didn't have enough customers to afford the luxury of firing the complainers or "kissing off" the excessively picayune. And they lacked the experience necessary to tap dance their way out of trouble, so no nit was too small to attend to when a customer picked at it. To this day, the rule at Miller Business Systems and Business Interiors is, "If the customer says it's a problem, it's a problem."

And when an employee said, "I have an idea for improving things around here," the Millers listened and learned, because as often as not that employee's idea was one idea more than either of them had had about the issue at hand. And it worked. More important, Jim Miller never forgot what he and Joan learned about listening to customers and employees in those scary, hand-to-mouth salad days: Never become too knowledgeable, experienced, or successful to have the humility and wisdom to listen, learn, and respond to customers and employees alike.

If that sounds, well, too simple to be true, it is. You see, there is a third fundamental element at the heart of the Miller Business Systems success story—Jim Miller himself and his unwavering belief in the power of people working together toward a common goal; his belief in, and wonder at, the power of teamwork.

When you and I watch team sports, we generally walk away marveling at the performance of one or two or three star players, enthralled by the million-dollar quarterback's passing or the rookie phenomenon forward's three-point shooting or the premier goalie's catlike reaction to the puck. Jim Miller walks away awed by the coordination and the flawless execution of complex game plans and the guarding and blocking and checking that made it possible for the "star players" to hit the jump shot, dive into the end zone, and be in the position to intercept the rocketing slap shot.

For Jim, the belief that truly marvelous and almost magical things can happen when people work in a coordinated, cooperative fashion toward a common goal does not end at the stadium gate. It carries over, undiminished, into his business dealings as well. Jim sees his colleagues at Miller Business Systems and Business Interiors as a team—and himself as a player/coach. And like every wise coach, Jim knows that the best game plan is only as good as the people executing it. Talented people, well trained and enthusiastically supported, rewarded, and recognized for their hard work and accomplishments make the Miller Business Systems and Business Interiors teams click.

As you read this account of the lessons in business team coaching that Jim Miller has learned through twenty-five years of success, remember one other thing: Jim Miller loves his work and it shows. It shows in the way he walks into the building in the morning. It shows in the buoyant way he greets and the quiet, attentive way he listens to and makes time for his associates. It shows in the energetic way he converses with customers and peers and anyone who shows an interest in the business and his manager/coach ideas. And, perhaps hidden in the day-to-day actions of this fireball that is Jim Miller, is the most important message of all: Without love and enthusiasm for what you're doing and respect and admiration for the people you are doing it with, the best management techniques in the world are worth little.

The success story of an enterprise like Miller Business Systems begins in the heart of the coach or it doesn't begin at all.

—Ron Zemke

# Introduction

# Why I Learned to Park on a Hill

> *"Whose turn is it to push the Volkswagen?"*

"AND WHAT else may I help you with this morning?" my wife asked one of our first customers as she laid her armful of legal pads on the counter.

"Oh, yes. I need a bottle of Liquid Paper. White."

Having grown up in Wisconsin, all Joan could envision was a liquid form of wood pulp before it becomes paper. They bottled that stuff?

"Just a moment, please." With anything but a confident look, she scurried to the stockroom to ask one of our three employees for help.

The employee just stared at her in wonder. "You mean you just bought an office-supply store and you don't even know what Liquid Paper is?"

That's just what we'd done. We scraped together our total net worth (which was twelve thousand dollars) by selling the house, the lawn mower, the cars, the kids' piano—anything that had monetary value—and borrowing on our life insurance. Adding a twelve-thousand-dollar loan from my father, we had moved from Green Bay, Wisconsin, to Arlington, Texas, to buy a business on the verge of bankruptcy. A business that was doing only fifty thousand dollars in annual sales.

It took two days just to learn where everything was and what we

3

had in inventory. On the third day at the store, I took the three wary, down-at-the-mouth employees who "came with the business" to lunch and made a pact with them. "I know that the three of you are already looking for jobs. In fact, considering how this place was run, I can't blame you. But stay with me and you'll be proud you work here." They agreed to give me a chance.

And so my first *team* was born.

I have always thought in terms of teams, and teamwork, when it comes to work. In part, it comes from playing on school teams when I was growing up in Milwaukee. But I think the real reason is deep down inside I might be a frustrated coach. I've coached company teams that played after work and I was coaching church and Little League teams long before I became a parent.

Over the years I have found that I seem to have an ability to get people to pull together as a team. And I never had a bigger challenge than the one I faced the day that I took those three employees to lunch. They explained that the company's reputation for poor service left customers buying from us only as a last resort. The second week at the store, we brought a radio to work, just so there would be a little noise in the place. We figured that with the radio, the store would seem more lively.

Our immediate goal was trying to survive. Our game strategy was to go out and become active in the community and to secure new accounts. Deciding on that game strategy was simple. If you hope to stay in business but have no money for advertising and no sales force, you don't have any choice other than to become known in the community, knock on doors yourself, and ask people for their business.

My playing field would be Arlington, Texas, right in the heart of the Dallas–Fort Worth metroplex. The only "athletic" equipment that came with the business happened to be a very beat-up delivery truck and an old Volkswagen that wouldn't start without a push.

Where to start? Well, I had worked for a large business-forms company prior to purchasing our store. I knew that Reynolds and Reynolds, a business-forms company that I used to compete against in Wisconsin, had an office nearby. I called the purchasing agent and invited him to lunch.

Knowing that the Volkswagen wouldn't start if I ever killed the engine, I pulled into the parking lot of his office building and left the motor running while I went in to get him. When we came back out and he saw the idling Volkswagen, my prospect looked surprised.

"Hey, you left your engine running," he said.

"Really? Guess I forgot to shut it off."

Slightly embarrassed, I climbed behind the wheel and we headed off to lunch. At the restaurant, I parked the car and shut off the ignition. What the heck. If he gave me an order, I'd figure out some way to get it started later.

During lunch, I told him about buying the store and about my plans for using my team of three to turn the business around. Finally, I popped the question: "Who are you buying your office supplies from?"

"A firm over in Dallas," he replied. "But I'd just as soon buy from you. You're local and I like your enthusiasm."

A new customer! I was thrilled. Things were looking up. We left the restaurant and he climbed into the Volkswagen with me for the lift back to his office. Under my breath, I prayed for a mechanical miracle. Nothing. Just the grinding. That awful grinding that I'd come to expect—and hate.

Disgusted, I finally turned to the new customer. "Would you mind getting out and giving a little push to get it started?"

He climbed out and pushed the car until we heard the engine start. Having regained my composure by the time we got back to his office, I didn't want to let him get away without my having an order in hand.

"If you'll give me just a minute, I'll go inside with you and we'll write up the order," I said, reaching for the ignition.

"Hey, don't shut it off," he said with a big smile. "Just keep the thing running!" He jumped out and slammed the door and said, "I'll call you with the order this afternoon!" And he did.

That story is typical of our beginnings. In retrospect, what we went through in our early days—both at work, and when we first started meeting people in the community—was pretty funny.

Soon after we bought the store, one of our vendors decided we needed a dose of relaxation amidst our struggle for survival, so he graciously invited us to a dinner dance at a prestigious country club in Dallas.

Our only problem—how to get there! The choices weren't promising: the Volkswagen that refused to start without a push, or our delivery truck that had bald tires, a dented body, a big crack in the

windshield, and no passenger seat. When you are just about bankrupt, buying good—or even adequate—transportation doesn't get
a high priority. You just want to survive.

Considering my recent experience with the Volkswagen, we
opted for the truck. I figured I could put a folding chair on the
passenger's side for Joan. Of course, this was before the mandatory
seat-belt laws. So, as we turned a corner, or hit the brakes, she'd
have to hold on to the dashboard to keep the chair from sliding
around. But at least I was fairly certain the thing would start, and
we hoped to park down the street from the country club so no one
would see how we arrived.

You guessed it—they had valet parking. In her beautiful formal
dress, Joan climbed out of the truck from her folding chair in front
of a multitude of people. We still laugh when we think of their
reactions.

Even our three children paid the price for my decision. Many
mornings you'd hear the following conversation around the breakfast table:

"Whose turn is it to push the Volkswagen today? I have to go to
work."

"Not mine."

"I did it yesterday."

"It's your turn today."

But Joan and I lay awake nights worrying about things more
serious than a temperamental car or dilapidated delivery truck.

Problems like cash flow, for example.

Naively believing the ubiquitous "Your check is in the mail," I
made hourly trips to the post office as I began the balancing act
performed on a tightrope between debits and credits. After a while,
the folks at the post office took pity on me.

"You know," one of the clerks told me after I made my fourth
trip to check our post office box that day, "by nine A.M. we stop
putting mail in the boxes. If it's not there by then, it is not going to
be there that day."

That left more time to work on gaining new customers, keeping
the ones we had happy, and wondering if we would ever be able to
expand beyond our small storefront in downtown Arlington.

But twenty-five years later, I can report that *I* didn't make a go
of it. *My team* did.

From previous jobs as a sales rep and sales manager, I understood the enthusiasm for, the value of, and the payoff that comes from the team concept in selling. Using the team concept to win back dissatisfied customers, keep them happy, and inspire a company during difficult financial times is what I've spent the last twenty-five years doing with our employees.

Now, I am not the first person who has discovered the importance of teamwork, nor am I the first to turn customer service into a passion. Just as quality and excellence were on every corporate tongue in the 1980s, teamwork, service, and partners in progress have become the 1990s theme. Companies big and small have all seen the numbers compiled by the White House Office of Consumer Affairs:

- For every customer who bothers to complain, there are twenty-six others who remain silent.
- The average "wronged" customer will tell eight to sixteen people.
- Some 91 percent of unhappy customers will never buy from you again.
- It costs about five times as much money to get a new customer as it costs to keep a current one.

But while everybody has seen these numbers, and a lot of people talk a good game, very few people go out and play the game the way our people do. How we do it is what I want to share with you.

For too long, managers and business owners have focused on the *sales team* to the exclusion of the *support team* in the attempt to satisfy their customers. That's the wrong game plan, the wrong game entirely for business in the nineties.

Customer service begins when the sales reps leave the field. The salespeople make the promises; that's what *gets* the customer. But the support staff are the people who have to *keep* the customer.

The salespeople's promises may make a short-term sale, but the players behind the scenes turn that one-time buyer into a long-term customer. The delivery drivers, the installers, the order processors, the invoicing clerks—they are all part of the team that makes things happen for the customer.

That's the reason we have been successful so far.

That's the reason we have been able to grow from a $50,000 company twenty-five years ago to a $150 million company today. We have grown from our original location in Arlington to include Dallas–Fort Worth, Houston, San Antonio, Austin, and Waco.

Teamwork—*everyone* working together—has made it possible.

# What's Teamwork?

> *Coming together is a beginning, staying together is progress, and working together as a team is success.*

BEFORE I go further, let me explain what I mean by teamwork. This book is not about personality quirks; it's about spirit, attitude, and enthusiasm. It's about how you can get everyone to work together toward the same goal.

The clearest example of teamwork that we all identify with is, not surprisingly, in sports. When a team—and it doesn't matter what type of team—pulls together, it usually wins. I think most people understand that, even if they never played sports as kids, and never looked at a newspaper sports section in their lives. Sports metaphors in the business world have long been used for emphasis and motivation. Even if you hate playing sports, you've learned the basics by osmosis.

At our companies, corporate teamwork is a structured concept, and one that applies in every department in the companies. Our teams—and our six hundred employees are divided into dozens of them—compete against other teams within the company, or against performance standards or goals they set for themselves.

Regardless of the reward, whether it be money, trips, tickets to the ball game or ballet, gasoline paid for a month, days off with pay, jewelry, or just keeping your job, the teamwork philosophy promotes camaraderie and a win-win situation for all concerned.

# The Payoff Is Promising

**W**HAT EXACTLY are the payoffs of that win-win situation? The section headings of this book give you a pretty good idea:

- Satisfied customers
- Innovative ideas
- Quality products and services
- Increased sales and profits
- Solutions to problems
- Employee loyalty and reduced turnover
- Fun

If those are the benefits, why don't all companies and departments within them field teams?

I think there are several reasons:

- *Many don't understand the concept.* To them teamwork means simply participative management, a concept that is usually just given lip service. You'll hear a few "atta boys" when a salesperson lands an account, but that's about it.
- *Many are threatened by loss of authority or control.* If people are working together as a team, the people in

charge say to themselves, "Then what are the managers supposed to do?" They never realize that every team needs a captain, a coach, *and* a manager.

- *Many don't ever find the time.* These organizations and managers lurch from crisis to crisis. They never call time out, or get additional help in developing their game plan.
- *Many don't know how.* They don't know how to create a team, choose team leaders, or create a compensation system that rewards the whole team.

What you hold in your hands is what I hope will become your *playbook* for creating, nurturing, and rewarding the members of your team. It is a guide to building a better company, and getting the people who work with you more involved with their jobs and their company. If you implement some of these ideas, your employees will start saying, "Put me in, coach." "Give me the ball." "Let me help." "What can I do?"

Specifically, what's the payoff?

Large organizations will be able to revamp their divisions or departments to instill reliability and accountability. Small-business owners will be able to build a reputation as the best in their industry.

In both cases, work will become more *profitable*—and definitely more fun.

If I'm making success sound easy, it isn't. If I'm making it sound reasonable and logical, it is.

A winning team in business demands just exactly what it demands on the playing field, and that is:

- Coaching to win
- Scouting the competition
- Devising a game strategy
- Anticipating constantly
- Selecting competent players
- Holding drills
- Scheduling scrimmages
- Critiquing performance
- Giving pep talks
- Working the clubhouse
- Learning from the losses

- Recruiting constantly
- Developing strong reserves
- Using the media successfully
- Developing a coaching staff
- Celebrating the wins

### *Let's play ball.*

# PART 1

# Customer Service: Teams Keep Customers Happy

# Whose Rules Do You Play By?

> *The road to success is always under construction.*

SOME COMPANIES set the rules; they tell customers how to play the game. Other companies ask customers what they'd like the rules to be; then they do everything possible to play by those rules. The difference in those two attitudes separates the excellent service companies from the average and poor ones.

If you want to succeed today, you have to play by the customers' rules.

Many companies don't do that. In fact, not only do they expect you to always play by their rules, they're rude in explaining what those rules are. Here's what I mean.

A manager we hired, who had just moved to the area, took an armful of suits into one of the local dry cleaners, explaining that he needed to have them back the next morning.

"They won't be ready until after six P.M.," the woman behind the counter snapped.

"That'll be too late, because I'm leaving town at five o'clock," the manager said. "Couldn't I get them earlier?"

The woman shook her head. "That's it," she said, in a voice that made it clear that the customer was being a pest. "They'll be ready after six."

The manager lifted his suits off the counter, and put them back under his arm. As he walked out the door, he heard the woman say with a sarcastic tone, "I hope you'll be happy somewhere else."

He was. He found a dry cleaner a few blocks away who was more than willing to make the extra effort to get his suits back when he needed them. He has been going to that dry cleaner ever since.

Didn't the woman at the first store understand that the new customer probably represented twelve hundred dollars a year in business? That's exactly how you have to look at every potential customer. What's important is not how much business the person is going to do with you today. After all, whether or not the store cleaned that manager's suits wouldn't make a lot of difference to the cleaner's earnings this year. The real value of a customer is how much he might spend with you over the course of a lifetime.

The customer that the woman alienated represented twelve hundred dollars in business the first year, and the next, and the year after that. She wasn't turning down a chance to make twenty dollars from cleaning a couple of suits. She was turning down twelve thousand dollars over the next ten years.

But she didn't look at the potential customer that way. Many businesses don't—and it costs them.

Here's another example. The CEO of a large Dallas company took a customer to dinner at a local restaurant. He repeatedly tried to catch the waiter's eye so they could have their iced tea glasses refilled, but the waiter never looked their way. Frustrated, the executive marched into the kitchen, got the iced tea pitcher, and filled the glasses himself.

The next day, he contacted the manager of the restaurant to complain. But the manager, just like the waiter, didn't seem to care if the customer was happy.

The executive cared, though. He cared a lot. Right then he told the manager that he was canceling a dinner for 275 that his company had scheduled at that restaurant and was going someplace else.

One last example. One of our sales managers had been traveling for a while, and hadn't had time to buy a present to take to an upcoming wedding. On his way to the reception, he stopped at a department store, picked out a gift, took it to the cashier, and asked to have it wrapped.

"I'm sorry," said the woman behind the counter. "You'll have to take it to the gift-wrapping department, and they are all backed up now. It will take them about an hour to get to it."

"I'm running a little late," the manager said. "How about selling me the paper, and I'll wrap it myself?"

"That's against our policy. You'll just have to wait."

The sales manager put his gift back on the shelf, left the store, and went to another department store down the street. They gladly wrapped the gift he purchased from them while he waited, and he was on his way to the wedding.

You can imagine where he will do his shopping in the future.

## THE GUY WHO BROUGHT THE BAT AND BALL MAKES THE RULES

*Listen, be flexible, and respond.*

Do you remember when you used to play sand-lot ball games? The guy who brought the bat and ball set the rules. He decided what to use for boundaries, who chose sides, and which team would bat first.

Our companies believe the customer owns the bat and balls.

We have something like 9,216 service options. We'll literally do whatever the customer wants, to the best of our ability. Consider:

- If customers need furniture installed during nonbusiness hours, we'll work at night, early in the morning, or on weekends.
- If customers want monthly usage reports in a format different from the one we usually use, we'll send someone over to sit down with them to see what information is needed, and how they'd like it formatted. From then on, that's exactly how they'll get their reports.
- How can customers order? They can use *our* forms. They can use *their* forms. They can *call* us, *fax* us, or

order *computer-to-computer.* They can use *our* stock number or *theirs.* If they can't place their order during our normal business hours, our rep will phone them at 2:00 A.M. (and we have some customers who keep that kind of schedule!) to discuss their needs.

• If customers don't like our delivery carts rolling across their light-colored carpets, we'll hand-carry their merchandise.

• We routinely deliver to one central receiving point. But one customer wanted items delivered to multiple locations. The question wasn't *"Are* we going to do it?" The question was *"How* are we going to do it?"

Does the customer pay for the additional services? Sometimes; it depends on the nature of the request and the cost involved. If it is something that is going to require us to spend a lot of money, then we'll charge the customer what it costs us.

For example, a customer hadn't budgeted furniture money until July, but he needed delivery in April. So we worked out a deal where we ordered the furniture early and rented it to him for three months until his new budget went into effect.

## HATE TO SAY NO

We hate to say no to customers—about anything they feel they really need.

Before you shake your head no to a customer, rethink the rules. Why can't you be flexible?

Why can't you extend office hours, if your customers like to shop after work?

Why can't you offer leasing as well as purchasing?

Why can't you deliver?

Why can't you come in early? Stay late?

Why can't you use their requisition number?

Why can't you keep records of customer purchases?

Why can't you take reservations?

Why can't you . . . ? You fill in the blanks with whatever your customers ask for.

Most customers will pay for customizing, for convenience, for quality, for value. They are willing to pay for flexibility, if it meets their needs.

We will do just about anything they want, short of our absolutely losing money on the deal.

## OPEN WITH ''WHAT DO YOU NEED DONE?'' AND ''HOW MAY I HELP?''

As you can imagine, all this flexibility will mean extra effort, constant change, and attention to detail, especially from your operations people. Why would you go to all this trouble to land a new account?

I think there are lots of reasons. When potential customers get a phone call from a sales rep, they typically put up a wall of resistance. They're expecting *your* pitch. *Your* rules. *Your* policies. They're primed to resist. If you start with "What do you need, and how may we help you," you'll totally disarm them.

Have your entire sales team and customer-service team memorize this line: *"Tell me exactly what you want and consider it done."* Listen to what your customers, or potential customers, say in response to that, and then do what they want.

If your employees understand that you are not in the business of just selling products, but rather in the business of solving a customer's problem and taking care of his or her needs, you'll be on the road to success.

For example, after a sales presentation to a major prospect in the computer-programming and equipment business, an officer of that company asked Mike Miller, president of Miller Business Systems, if he could furnish customized computer-usage reports for their company. Their current supplier could not furnish these reports. That afternoon Mike and the director of Information Systems created a computer program to provide exactly what the prospect requested. The information was sent overnight to the president of the firm. That company is now one of our largest accounts.

With "Tell me exactly what you want and consider it done" as a motto, you are letting customers know you care about pleasing them. You'll build repeat business, and consistently challenge your competition to keep up with you.

Plus, you're well down the road to creating customers for life. After customers have invested time in explaining what they want done—and had the opportunity to see exactly how you deliver on your promises—they'll be less likely to switch to a competitor.

With a company philosophy of *"Listen, be flexible, and respond,"* you identify yourself as a customer-driven service organization.

### COACH'S CHECKLIST

✔ *Be flexible.* The customer doesn't need to learn how you do business; *you* need to learn how the customer wants to do business with you. Customers own all the bats and balls. They choose which team to play on, and they can go home anytime they want.

✔ *Disarm prospects with "Tell me exactly what you need and consider it done!"* Once they tell you, make sure you deliver it to them.

✔ *Never say no to a customer,* unless you are going to lose a lot of money by saying yes.

# 2

# Assume Nothing; Ask Everything

| "Are we all singing out of the same hymn book?" |
| --- |

WHEN CUSTOMERS decide they don't need a $6.99 item they ordered, it's cheaper to tell them to keep it—no charge—than to have a driver make an extra stop to pick it up.

But we pick up that unwanted item anyway. Why? Customer perception.

One of the ways we try to stay in touch with our customers is by annually sending them surveys. We want to know what they like about doing business with us, and what they don't. In the past on those surveys, customers frequently wrote: "Delivery drivers are slow to pick up returns."

In our eyes, we weren't slow to pick up returns; we didn't intend to pick up anything that cost $7.50 or less. Our policy—as we consistently told our customers—was to issue a credit memo and let them keep the item with our compliments. For the small amount of money involved, we figured that made good business sense.

Good business sense for us, maybe. But it wasn't good business as far as our customers were concerned, as the notes on our surveys indicated. Even though we weren't charging them for the merchandise, the customer still wanted us to come pick it up.

I didn't understand why, but I finally got a chance to find out at one of the focus-group luncheons we hold. Just like the surveys, asking customers to lunch periodically to talk about how well we are taking care of their needs is another way of making sure our customers are happy with the job we're doing for them.

Before these focus-group luncheons, we always send an agenda to the people who are invited, so they know exactly the kinds of things we want to find out. We ask them to talk to their staff before they come, so they can find out exactly how well we are taking care of their firm's needs. We also want to know what other areas, not listed on the agenda, should be addressed.

Topics discussed at these lunches change from focus group to focus group. One time, we'll discuss how easy it is to order from us, and at another focus group we might talk about how well our delivery system is meeting their needs. But no matter what the topic is, we always make sure to ask the same open-ended questions: "What could we do better in providing service to your firm?" "Is another firm doing something better than we are?" "Is there anything that bothers you about doing business with us?"

"There sure is," came the reply at one lunch. "When are you going to pick up the merchandise we don't want and give us a credit?"

We explained that they had already been credited, and why it was cheaper, from our point of view, just to let them keep the item. No charge.

"But I don't want it on my desk! Every time I look at it, I get upset, plus you louse up our bookkeeping. I want you to pick it up!"

Our drivers now pick up returns—even if it costs us money to do so. We thought we were being good guys by letting the customers keep the items at no charge. Our customers didn't. And only the customer's opinion matters.

Here's another example. We try to keep our customers informed of items our suppliers are putting on sale, and new products that are being introduced that could increase their efficiency. We include product fliers with all orders. Most of our customers appreciate this service.

Most, but not all. We got a call recently from a purchasing agent at a company where we have done business for a long time.

"Hey, please, don't stuff fliers in our orders," he said. "With over five thousand employees, we don't want each one deciding what product to order. *We'll* decide what new products our employees need to see."

"You've got it," we told them. No fliers in their orders.

Will customers tell you where and how you fouled up, right after you've paid for their filet mignon at a focus-group lunch? They definitely will.

Now, some customers are going to be hesitant to bring up "little things," so you've got to assure them that you want to know about the little things as well as any major problems they might be having.

After each focus luncheon, we send customers a recap of discussions at the luncheon and continue to update them until everything they were concerned about is resolved.

When your customers know you really care about quality service, they'll talk to you about their small dissatisfactions—issues they'd never even mention to an organization unless they're convinced it is committed to outstanding service.

To make sure they do tell us, we've learned not to assume anything about what customers want or don't want. *We ask.* And we ask in several different ways: we hold focus groups; our employees ask day in and day out, when they are out in the field; and we survey constantly (something we will talk about shortly).

But do you know which employees bring us customer intelligence the quickest? Our drivers. They are out talking to customers every day. More important, they can tell us whether a customer is being called on by one of our competitors, or which customers are unhappy with the service they are getting from another firm.

Our drivers pass along all the market information they gather, and we meet with them once a month just so they know how important they are to our business. They are an extension of our sales force, and they are very valuable members of our team.

## EXPLAINING WHY IS EASY; CHANGING IS DIFFICULT

All this interaction with the customer breaks us of the habit of assuming.

Perhaps the thing that helps the most is the surveys we send out. By surveys, I don't mean those two- or three-sentence, "How do you feel about us today?" cards. There is a place for those too, as I'll explain later. It would be easy to read those cards and simply explain away any negative comments: "No wonder we were slow to respond; we had three people out sick that day." Or, "Our vendors fouled up the paperwork again; that's really what the customer is complaining about." Explanations are easy. Committing to change is difficult.

If you are going to change, you have to know what to change, and sending out a 3 × 5-inch index card that asks a couple of questions simply won't give you enough information. That's why we randomly select customers every year and use a six-page survey that prompts people to comment on all aspects of our services—from delivery times to accuracy of invoices. The check-the-appropriate-box form doesn't take more than ten minutes for the customer to complete. But it does require thoughtful answers.

Will customers take the time to tell you what they think? The majority do. We get a phenomenal 56 percent response rate. Most companies would be thrilled if they got a tenth of that.

The reason I think we get so many people to respond is that we use a third party to collect, tabulate, and report the data to us. That shows our customers that we are serious about this survey. "If they put that kind of expense and effort into the project," our customers say, "then they are likely to pay attention to the results."

One strategy we use, to know which customers respond, is to put the space for the individual's name and the company name at the top of the first page of the survey form. We've found that better than 90 percent fill in their names using this method, as compared to a 70 percent response when the names appear at the end of the form.

If customers take the time to tell you what they want, they expect you to listen and take action.

And we do.[1]

Specifically, we pay attention to our customers' *needs* and *expectations*.

The credit memo issued to the customer for the unwanted item represents a need; the pickup of the merchandise represents an

---

1. If you don't want to pay an outside firm, swap surveys with another company that has a customer base the size of yours. You handle their surveys, and they'll handle yours. Or you can ask a vendor to do it for you. They will probably say yes, because they appreciate your business.

expectation. (The customer expects the merchandise to be picked up if they don't want it.) Failure on either score can be your downfall. Unsatisfactory scores in either category means you are going to have to change the way you do business.

Take our catalog, for example. On one survey, several customers commented that our wholesaler's catalog confused them. Specifically, they said the products were difficult to locate. So we went back to that wholesaler and asked what they could do to improve things. They made cosmetic changes, but they really didn't do much.

On the next survey, we got the same comments: "Your catalog is hard to use. The products are difficult to find."

We went back to the wholesaler again, but nothing really changed. So *we* changed—to a different wholesaler, one who had a catalog that satisfied our customers. To sever ties with our original wholesaler was difficult, because we had enjoyed doing business with that company for almost ten years. But as a customer-oriented company, we had no choice.

If customers take the time to tell you what they want, they expect you to *listen* and *take action,* and both those things are important.

## Don't Forget Off-the-Cuff Reactions

As good as long surveys are, there are advantages to using shorter ones as well. The biggest advantage is that you can use the shorter surveys as a spot check to see how well you are doing day to day. Although in-depth surveys will give you more detailed information, you can't send out a six-page survey with every order. After a while, customers will stop filling them out.

However, a postcard-sized survey that asks, "Did this order arrive on time? Was the invoice correct? Was the salesperson professional and courteous? Did the installer do their job right?" will usually get answered.

These shorter surveys accomplish several things. First, they show the customer that you care. Second, they serve as a spot check on how well you are doing. Third, they give you a chance to correct *immediately* whatever problems there are.

And that is the important thing about surveys. *You have to respond to the customers if they have taken the time and trouble to answer your questions.*

When we recently received a survey card with every category checked below the satisfactory level, our company president, Mike Miller, personally called the customer to determine what the problem was. We had flat-out missed our delivery date. It doesn't happen often, but unfortunately it still happens on occasion.

Mike called, found out that we had made a major mistake, wrote the customer a letter of apology, and sent flowers as an added touch. Later, the customer told her sales rep she was amazed, and appreciated that the president of the company cared. Not only did we not lose the account, their ordering from us has actually increased. It's now one of our best accounts.

Customers need assurance that you're not surveying just for the sake of patting yourselves on the back, but because you are truly looking for ways to improve your service to them. So we take great pains to do just that.

Every single person who responds to a survey gets a personal response from us. If a response is negative, we will either visit or phone the customers to find out exactly what the problem is, and then do everything in our power to set things right.

At Business Interiors, a call is also made to customers who mark their survey cards "good" or "excellent." We've found some great information from customers who view us as excellent. They appreciate the fact that someone called them, just as much as the customer who marked a "fair" or "poor" square. In addition, we give our customers progress reports about what action we are taking to implement their suggestions.

A few years ago our customers wanted to know why we didn't offer printing services in addition to office supplies and furniture. The trend in the nineties is to do business with fewer suppliers to help reduce paperwork costs. Our customers were pleased with our service and requested that we expand our service to include printing, which we did.

It seems that everybody and his brother is trying to survey customers today. We get a higher response rate to our surveys than most, because customers know we are going to take what they say seriously, act on it, and keep them informed of what we are doing.

If you are not comfortable designing the surveys yourself, or you are not sure you'll be able to interpret the results correctly, then hire a professional to do the surveys for you. They can be a real help in making sure the surveys will be sent to the right people, and that your questions will get to the heart of the issues you are concerned about. The short survey card that we have successfully used is shown below.

---

*We are on a Quest for Excellence!*
*Please tell us how we are doing.*

MILLER BUSINESS SYSTEMS, INC.
**QUEST** FOR EXCELLENCE

Company _____
Your Name _____
Telephone _____ / _____

| | EXCELLENT | GOOD | POOR |
|---|---|---|---|
| Was your order taken promptly? | ☐ | ☐ | ☐ |
| Was our catalog helpful with your selection? | ☐ | ☐ | ☐ |
| Did you receive your order when expected? | ☐ | ☐ | ☐ |
| Was the order filled and packed correctly? | ☐ | ☐ | ☐ |
| Overall rating of Miller's service? | ☐ | ☐ | ☐ |

Suggestions: _____
_____
_____

---

## YOU STILL HAVE TO DO MORE

Focus groups and surveys are great ways of finding out what customers want, but you can't stop there. We once lost a large account because no one from our management had been in *personal* contact with their management in quite some time. Because we don't ever want that to happen again, we have developed our Key Account Program.

Volume is not the only way we determine a key account. *Key accounts* are: large local companies; companies that are part of Fortune 500; companies that are part of our national American

**Key Account Review**

Customer _____ Date _____

Account Executive _____ Location _____

Miller Business Systems Reps.:          Customer Reps.:

_____       _____

_____       _____

_____       _____

Customer Comments on Service Quality:

_____

_____

_____

_____

_____

_____

Opportunities for Growth: _____

_____

_____

_____

Action Items: 1. _____

2. _____

3. _____

4. _____

General Comments: _____

_____

_____

Office Products Distributors (AOPD); and companies with ten or more national locations.

Someone *in management* is assigned to each of those accounts in addition to the team that takes care of this customer on a day-to-day basis.

We make "management-to-management" calls quarterly. The Key Account Review form (shown on page 28) is completed by each manager. The forms are reviewed by the vice president of sales and marketing.

There are many advantages to doing this. First, it is another way to show the customer you care. Second, it further cements your relationship with the customer. If a manager of our company is in constant contact with a vice president of their company, and our executive is doing everything in his or her power to satisfy the customer, it is less likely that the customer is going to switch to another supplier.

## Assumptions Will Kill You

Everything we have talked about is designed to ensure that customers are happy. And you even have to check that they're happy when you think you are doing them a favor.

Here's an example. After one of our Business Interiors customers received a furniture quote, he changed his mind about a few desks he wanted. We reprinted the quote and sent it again. A couple of days later, he changed his mind about the style of chairs. We reprinted the quote. A day later, he decided on a new color scheme. To speed up the whole process, we told him just to line through the unwanted items and hand-write the new order numbers and prices. No, no, no. He wanted us to redo and reprint the entire quote. We did—through several more changes.

Each time, we offered to speed up the process by simply inking in the items. Each time, he grew a little more exasperated. By talking to him, we finally got the full picture. His boss consistently yelled about his inattention to detail and his sloppy reports and paperwork. As a result, the main thing he wanted from us was *not* accurate quotes and a speedy delivery, but impeccably neat paperwork (which went to his boss). He didn't consider our offer to handle the paperwork informally a favor; to him it was a liability. It would have made him look bad in front of his boss.

Assumptions can put you in the poorhouse. And most times you don't have to assume. All you have to do is *ask*. If you're receptive—if you constantly ask people what they want through day-to-day contact, surveys, focus groups, and any other device you can think of—customers will tell you exactly what they want.

If you are willing to listen, you won't have to assume anything.

The following lists some of the questions you might want to ask in order to find out exactly what your customers want. You'll notice all the questions are open-ended. That's important. You don't want customers to just answer "yes" or "no"—you are really trying to find out how they feel about doing business with you.

Here's what we ask:

- How well do we deliver what we promise?
- How often are we on time with projects/deliveries?
- What difficulties do you have in reaching us with problems?
- Do you know what other products/services we offer?
- How flexible are we in meeting your special requirements?
- How courteous is our staff?
- How well do we make an effort to understand your business operations and needs?
- How would you rate the quality of our products?
- How would you rate our service overall on a scale of one to five?
- How do we compare to our competitors in service?
- Would you recommend us to your friends?
- What are three changes that would make it easier for you to do business with us?

The purpose behind all these questions is not just to find out what we did "wrong." Sure, we want a chance to correct our mistakes, but the real reason we ask all these things is to make sure that we don't assume *anything* about what our customers want.

Consider again that last question on our list, the one that asks: What are three changes that would make it easier for you to do business with us? You might be surprised how you could profit from the answer. For example, as a direct result of asking customers that question, we've installed a new phone system so that customers can call their customer-service rep directly rather than going through a central switchboard. We've also added more in-bound fax lines for customers to place orders. We changed our catalog, installed phones in our furniture-delivery trucks, and much, much more.

Ask customers what they want and then deliver it.

## SAY THANKS

> *The two most forgotten words in the English language are "thank you."*

If customers are nice enough to respond to your questions about what they want, be sure to thank them. We say thanks to customers at our focus luncheons by giving them an expensive pen and pencil set and a copy of Ron Zemke's book *The Service Edge*. Some companies take the names of everyone who responds, put them in a hat, and draw out the name of one customer who receives an elaborate gift. Do whatever you can afford, but thank your customers and remind them they'll hear from you about what you are going to do to implement their suggestions.

That's vital. *You must take action on their suggestions.*

Many entrepreneurial companies, as well as big organizations, focus on acquiring new customers at the expense of keeping current customers happy. That just doesn't make sense. It costs about five times as much money to attract a new customer as it costs to keep current customers.

Keeping customers happy is not easy, but we have a 98 percent customer-retention rate. The reason? We *listen* to what our customers want, and then do our best to give it to them. The expense and effort in getting feedback proves minimal when you think about long-term customers rather than short-term sales.

Be passionate about acting on customer feedback. Make customers feel that your company is really their company, make them feel like they are the only customer you have, and that you exist to make them happy.

## COACH'S CHECKLIST

✓ *Don't assume you know what customers want.* Ask them. In every conversation you have with them—through surveys, focus groups, and every other way you can think of.

✓ *Ask about the "little things."* Sure, you want to hear about the major changes your customers would like to have you make, but often it is the little things that will keep them happy.

✓ *Don't just listen . . . react.* Act on the things your customers tell you they want done. Provide progress reports on how you are doing toward implementing their suggestions.

✓ *Say "Thank you!"* Never take your customers for granted and remember to thank them for their business.

# Avoid Telling Outrageous Customer-Service Stories

> *Don't give customers heartburn.*

CUSTOMER LOYALTY rests on two issues: Doing *what* you say you will, *when* you say you will.

If we promise a customer 500 items at $3.19 each, he or she doesn't want to get an invoice for 500 items at $3.29 each, or even $3.20. If we say we're going to install 3,300 workstations in six weeks, the customer expects us to install 3,300—not 3,100—workstations in six weeks—or less.

*Consistent performance* and *kept promises.* That's what creating customers who will stay with you for life is all about.

Customers want you to be reliable and consistent. Products and services are too complex to research annually, and negotiations with new suppliers are time-consuming and expensive. Customers don't want to be constantly forced to switch to someone new, or something else. They want a reason to stick with you.

The best reason we can give them to stay is that we try to consistently *under-promise* and *over-deliver.*

Taking this approach to business is something we learned the hard way. Let me tell you a story that brought the lesson home to us.

One of our major customers merged with a larger company and needed to set up a new department for approximately two hundred employees. They called Business Interiors, our furniture company, with an immediate requirement to secure a lot of used furniture. To make matters worse, they wanted all the furniture to match. This included workstations, chairs, and files. Their lead time was only two weeks, which would have been an impossible task for most suppliers.

John Sample, president of Business Interiors, promised the unbelievable feat. He said he would locate matching used-furniture pieces from all over the nation and would install it all within a two-week period.

Everybody who knows the furniture business knows John had set himself an impossible task. It typically would take months to come up with all the furniture needed. Nevertheless, John scoured the nation like a hawk scavenging for food to coordinate furniture styles, colors, and design.

It was far from easy. Over the phone, firms would say their three desks matched, but when we received the shipment, we would find they didn't. Some shipments came in damaged and had to be refurbished on site.

But within fourteen days, we had located and installed thousands of pieces of furniture for the customer. All but five workstations were complete. Incredible. *Mission Impossible* turned possible. We were jubilant.

And the customer? The customer was disappointed.

We'd promised to have everything complete and delivered in two weeks. The customer didn't care that John and his team had been working around the clock and had basically accomplished the impossible within those fourteen days. All the customer knew was that we promised they would have *all* the furniture in fourteen days—and they didn't, as five workstations weren't complete until four days later. They didn't care that some of the firms who had promised us matching furniture in good condition didn't live up to their end of the bargain. They expected the merchandise to be there within two weeks; anything else represented failure in their eyes.

You have to *exceed* customer expectations. Every time. Always. Customers expect you to say *exactly* what you mean and *do* exactly what you say. If there's any doubt that you can pull something off, under-promise so you can over-deliver. Otherwise, you run the risk of disappointing the customer, no matter what you do.

Our record in filling orders accurately is 99.8 percent. We have a 98 percent next-day fill rate on items customers purchase from our catalog. So does that mean we go around shouting from the rooftops that we give excellent service? Well, we do publicize our service performance facts, *but we stress exactly what they are.* We don't say we fill every order right, and we don't claim we ship every item the next day. That would be extremely risky.

Why? Because that 99.8 percent success rate on filling orders means that for every thousand customers, two find an error in what they receive. And those two don't care that 998 other customers received accurate orders. All they know is they placed an order, and we got it wrong.

So rather than spending time focusing on the 99.8 percent accuracy rate—and setting up the customer for extreme disappointment when, on those two occasions out of a thousand, we goof—we spend our time improving the systems that allowed those two errors to slip through. We work on better training for our employees, installing equipment with better technology, developing better teamwork, and constantly working toward achieving 100 percent accuracy.

## HAVE A BACK-UP SYSTEM FOR EVERYTHING

> *"Regardless of the situation, that's my job!"*

The only way you can achieve what you promise is through *teamwork*. Teams add back-up coverage and provide a checks-and-balances system.

It's that simple . . . and that complex.

We have customer-service teams that help catch potential errors by our salespeople. Let's say a salesperson promises a customer a green chair. And let's say that the customer-service rep who enters the order notices that the chair comes only in black. Rather than just deliver the chair as a "surprise," the rep calls the customer to ask whether they want the black chair or if they'd rather change the style of the chair to one that comes in green. Having someone other than the salesperson enter the order is a way of double-checking our work and making sure that the customer ends up happy.

Your back-up system might be as simple as a phone number. All our customers have a phone number to call if they want to know about the status of their order. Often just giving them a special phone number is all it takes to make them happy.

On occasion, I've personally served as the back-up system. A customer called saying that two flip charts and easels were to be delivered for a 2:00 P.M. management meeting. At 1:30 P.M., the driver hadn't arrived. I told the customer I'd be there before 2:00 P.M.—and there would be no charge for the order. Throwing the items in my car, I rushed to her office.

The chairman of the board delivering easels and flip charts? You bet. Why? Because we promised, and if we promised, we are going to do whatever it takes to satisfy the customer, no matter how big the order, or how much work is involved. That was my job. My title doesn't mean anything to the customer if we don't perform.

Years ago on a typically hot July day in Texas, with the temperature over 100 degrees, our warehouse manager came to see me one afternoon about one P.M. He had a problem.

"Coach [you can see we take this teamwork concept seriously], we've got an order for twenty desks, twenty executive chairs, forty side chairs, and twenty files. They want everything delivered before the end of the day."

"So what's the problem?" I asked. "Don't we have the items in stock?"

"We've got the stock, but we don't have the trucks or personnel available at this hour to get it delivered."

"So why not rent a truck?"

"But what good would that do? We don't have anyone available to drive the truck."

"Sure we do—you and me." As a team, the two of us delivered and installed the furniture that afternoon. That was *my job,* as the customer had a need, and we had to perform.

Granted, there's usually a better back-up system than the CEO—and in fact the situation I just described rarely happens. But it does happen. The point is this: If you promise, deliver. Put back-up systems in place to ensure that you can follow through.

The back-up system can be as simple as "Sally will cover for Joe when Joe is tied up," or it can be more elaborate. We've set up a separate division for rush deliveries, called Hot Shots, that handles orders that customers need *immediately.* That way we don't have to disrupt regular deliveries if a customer tells us he or she needs something in the next thirty minutes. But whether you go the formal or informal route, make sure you have a system in place to handle the unexpected. Above all, you want customers to know you are reliable.

Our "Just-in-Time" system is another one that has been put to the reliability test on numerous occasions. Several years ago, we began to push the stockless inventory service. The idea behind it is simple. "Why should our customers have to warehouse their office supplies?" we asked ourselves. We could serve as their stockroom. All they would have to do is call us, and we'd deliver anything in our catalog the next day. That would reduce our customers' storage costs, handling costs, and cut down on pilferage. And this service would also give them another reason for doing business with us.

The day after we'd signed a big contract with a large firm, some of the customer's department heads were concerned that we couldn't perform as we promised and give next-day delivery. In a panic situation, one particular department head called to place multiple orders, totaling more than fifty thousand dollars.

"You can deliver it tomorrow, right?" he asked.

Quite frankly, he looked at this as a test to see whether we would be able to meet his challenge. You could tell from his voice that he *knew* we wouldn't be able to deliver in time.

It took three trucks and nine warehouse people to process the order, but we did it. The customer was astonished, delighted—and unprepared for the delivery. We had to stack products in their hallways.

On occasion, we've had customers call our sales reps at home, after our offices are closed, to place an emergency order. If unable to get into our warehouse, the reps will go to any local store that's open to fill the order. They'll even buy from a competitor if they have to, and deliver the item at a loss, to maintain our promise of next-day delivery.

## BACK YOUR SERVICE OR PRODUCT NO MATTER WHO'S AT FAULT

Another equally important part of being reliable is standing behind your product or service—even when the mistake is the customer's fault.

One customer wanted a particular filing system installed. The manufacturer's rep told the customer exactly what type of filing cabinets he should buy. We knew the rep was wrong. We knew that the cabinets he was suggesting would never hold the weight of the files the customer was planning to place in the cabinets. But when we challenged the choice, the manufacturer's rep, the manufacturer, and the customer all assured us they knew what they were doing. All we had to do was deliver the filing cabinets and install them.

Our installers spent 340 work hours setting up the filing system, and before they left the site they showed the secretaries how to load the file drawers.

The next day the customer called. "These filing cabinets are no good. They fall over when you open the drawers."

Actually, the problem was with the choice of files that the manufacturer had recommended using. The customer, of course, wasn't satisfied and wanted an entirely new filing system. We disassembled everything, returned the cabinets and files to the manufacturer, reordered what the customer needed, rented them files in the interim, and then, once the new ones arrived, installed the new filing system, which was the one we had originally recommended.

Now, this clearly wasn't our fault. The manufacturer knew they had recommended the wrong system and that the mistake had cost us 340 installation hours—not to mention the delay in getting the customer what they really needed. But instead of passing the buck, we solved the problem. (We also charged the manufacturer for the 340 hours.)

Another example. A customer had just sold his business to a group of investors who would be meeting with him the next day to close the deal. He wanted to give them lacquered pens, imprinted with their names, to use at the signing ceremony. Producing these pens is normally a ten-day process, but we turned the job around in just eight hours. Just another deadline to meet. We advertise exceptional service, and if we advertise it, we'd better deliver.

You shouldn't brag about providing extraordinary service. It should become routine. Other requests that we handle routinely, and that other firms would consider unusual, include the following:

- Insurance agents and adjustors needed thousands of pens and legal pads at the site of an airplane crash at

the Dallas–Fort Worth airport. We delivered them
there in minutes.
- An oil company needed five hundred Roach Motels for
immediate delivery as their rep traveled to their various
off-shore oil rigs. We don't carry pest-control devices—
we deal in office supplies and office furniture—
but we came up with Roach Motels and delivered them
on time.
- A purchasing agent from one of our largest customers
called me at home on Memorial Day. The president of
his corporation had just called him to say that he
wanted a temperature clock for his swimming pool, and
he wanted it now; he had people coming to his house
for a pool party later that day. We were closed, and we
didn't stock the item anyway. Since it was a holiday, I
couldn't reach a wholesaler who could deliver it. I called
around until I found a pool-supply company that was open,
bought the temperature clock, and then delivered it
to the president's home before his guests arrived.

These customers gave us a chance to promise and perform—or
promise and choke. If you promise excellent service, you have to
give it. You can't waffle when the requests get tough. *To say you're
going to provide the exceptional, and then not perform will do irreparable harm.*

## LONE RANGERS RARELY MAKE IT

> *Teamwork makes it happen!*

If you are going to provide exceptional customer service, you'll
need teamwork. Lone Rangers rarely make it when it comes to
satisfying the customer. One person simply cannot do enough. Let
me give you a couple of examples.
 A large account ordered three thousand workstations, and they

needed them delivered and installed in less than six weeks. Normally, it can take months to fill an order this size. But someone at their company had forgotten to place the order until the very last minute, and they desperately needed those workstations within six weeks.

To get them the merchandise in time—and we did—our purchasing department had to disrupt their daily flow of scheduled work to transmit the rush order to the manufacturer. Then our service rep had to be in daily contact with the manufacturer to find out the status of the job. We had to go to our installers and have them revamp their schedules. And so it went, down the line. One person, or even one department, acting alone would not have been able to satisfy the customer. Departmental teams have to be committed to working together to pull off this kind of thing and still make sure they can take care of the regular work load.

Another customer specified weekend installation of several hundred workstations. They said we could start the installation at 5:00 P.M. on Friday, and work all weekend—nights too, if we wanted—but we had to be out by 7:00 A.M. Monday. If that's what they wanted us to do, then that's what we'd do.

On Friday, while double-checking the order, we discovered that some of the furniture had not been shipped from the manufacturer in New York. It was still sitting on their dock. What do you do when your reputation for service depends on reliability? We flew two installers to New York, and had them rent a truck. They picked up the furniture, drove all night, and were able to get back to Dallas in time to install it by late Sunday evening.

In another down-to-the-wire scenario, the first floor of a customer's new building wasn't complete on the date they asked us to install all their new office furniture, so we offered to keep the furniture in our warehouse. No, they said, they wanted it in their basement. So we stored it there, and then a thunderstorm dumped fourteen inches of rain on the area.

Their building flooded, which caused the sewer lines that ran through their basement to crack. A combination of sewer and rain water turned their basement into a huge wading pool three feet deep.

They called us, and within forty minutes we had a crew of twenty at the site, hauling furniture out of the smelly, soggy mess. There was no time for hip boots. No time for masks. No time for anything that would have made the job bearable. While our service people were calling the manufacturers to find out how to treat the joints, metal, and wood to minimize the damage, we saved the furniture. There was no downtime for the customer.

You couldn't pay people enough to wade around in sewer water when it wasn't their job. But, of course, our people knew that taking care of the customer is everybody's job. They showed up and literally bailed out the customer.

We couldn't have done this without *teamwork,* because *teamwork makes it happen!* Our acronym for teamwork is:

**T** *TOGETHER*—Working together rather than as an individual you can make things happen more easily and professionally.

**E** *EMPATHY*—For fellow employees; concern about their well-being.

**A** *ASSIST*—The ability and desire to help others when they need assistance.

**M** *MATURITY*—Be mature in handling problems and challenges in a positive, constructive manner.

**W** *WILLINGNESS*—To work with people throughout the company in a friendly, cooperative manner.

**O** *ORGANIZATION*—Be professionally organized to reduce crisis situations with the help of other employees and departments.

**R** *RESPECT*—For people you work with on a daily basis.

**K** *KINDNESS*—For all people you come in contact with.

## BUILD A BIG REPUTATION ON THE LITTLE THINGS

You don't just build a reputation on the big things—like walking around in sewer water. You build it on the little things as well.

A consultant called us from a small town outside our service area.

"I'm working on a client proposal," he said, "and if I don't get a toner cartridge for my printer, I won't get my proposal to them in time. And if I don't win this contract, I might not be able to make this month's payroll for my employees."

"You're a hundred miles beyond the point where our trucks deliver," our service representative told him, "but why don't I meet you halfway."

So at seven o'clock the next morning, she put the cartridge in her car and drove fifty miles to the designated shopping mall to meet a customer she'd never sold to before and possibly wouldn't again. Our hope is, of course, that the customer will remember what we did for him the next time he—or his clients—need office supplies or office furniture, and that he will recommend one of our firms. But there is no guarantee. If you've built your business around taking care of the customer no matter what, you don't wait until you have a guarantee. You just drive a hundred miles round-trip to deliver what the customer needs.

The little things *do* count. Here's a story that brought that home to me.

Recently, while in Chicago for a convention, we were having dinner with colleagues at the Conrad Hilton Towers Hotel's Buckinghams Restaurant. Several of the first-timers to the city were discussing what to do and see. Within a few minutes, our waiter approached the table with a magazine that outlined all the attractions of the city.

"I couldn't help but overhear your discussion, and I wanted to make sure you had a good time while you're here," he said.

Obviously pleased at this unexpected helpfulness, we left the restaurant recommending the place to everyone we met. The waiter's employer could not have paid for advertising that would have been as effective as all the praise we gave that restaurant during the convention.

Do customers notice the little things? Are customers more loyal over the long haul because we did everything in our power to make them happy? Evidently so. Two separate business books have identified us as having one of the highest customer-retention rates of any organization in the nation. Some 98 percent of the companies who do business with us once stay with us.

Why do we have this kind of success? Because we do *what* we say we will, *when* we say we will. And we do it by using teams. Sure, people make mistakes. Acts of God sometimes disrupt plans. Customers change their minds. Products fail. But teamwork between departments goes a long way toward increasing reliability.

Between our teams, and the fact that we always have a back-up system in mind to deliver on our promises if routine channels get clogged, we're able to take care of the customer.

Have I told you any outrageous customer-service stories here? No, not really. If you asked our employees for some outrageous customer-service stories, they'd scratch their heads in puzzlement. We don't use that term at all. The outrageous has become the ordinary. That's part of our business. That's a big reason why our customers stay with us.

### COACH'S CHECKLIST

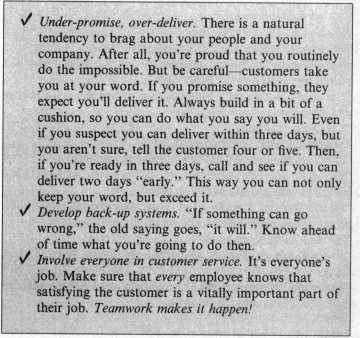

✔ *Under-promise, over-deliver.* There is a natural tendency to brag about your people and your company. After all, you're proud that you routinely do the impossible. But be careful—customers take you at your word. If you promise something, they expect you'll deliver it. Always build in a bit of a cushion, so you can do what you say you will. Even if you suspect you can deliver within three days, but you aren't sure, tell the customer four or five. Then, if you're ready in three days, call and see if you can deliver two days "early." This way you can not only keep your word, but exceed it.

✔ *Develop back-up systems.* "If something can go wrong," the old saying goes, "it will." Know ahead of time what you're going to do then.

✔ *Involve everyone in customer service.* It's everyone's job. Make sure that *every* employee knows that satisfying the customer is a vitally important part of their job. *Teamwork makes it happen!*

# 4

# Remember That Customers Buy the Whole Team

> *Never let an individual dominate a team.*

**H**OW MANY times has this happened to you?

"May I speak to Susan, please? I'd like to order some of the products we discussed the other day."

"I'm sorry but Susan's with another customer at the moment. May I have her call you?"

"Certainly. Thanks."

Two hours later, you call again.

"Is Susan available? I left her a message earlier."

"No, she's not. She's gone to lunch. Could you call back? Or, I'll leave her another message if you like."

"Okay. Thanks. I really need to get this project taken care of right away. Please have her call me as soon as possible."

The next morning, you call for the third time.

"I've still not received a call back from Susan Jones. I need to place an order."

"She's at a customer's site this morning until eleven. Didn't the two of you make contact yesterday?"

"No."

"Shall I leave her another message?"

"Oh . . . never mind. I'll call back."

Maybe you will, maybe you won't. Maybe you'll call a competitor instead.

Why do you have to go through all this?

It could be that Susan is just incredibly rude, but odds are that isn't the case. It could be that she was busy on a project; an emergency came up; she's incredibly backed up on work, or. . . . The list of possible reasons she didn't call back is almost endless.

So, why couldn't someone else at the company help you?

They probably could have, but you weren't crazy about that idea. When you call the hair salon, or the auto-repair shop, you like to deal with the same person every time, right? The one who knows you and your needs. Most customers share that feeling. They like to deal with people they know when they call to place an order or to check on its status.

So what happens when customers call and their customer-service rep is unavailable? Three alternatives: 1. They can wait, and wait, and wait. Until after lunch, until she gets off the phone, until she returns from vacation. 2. They can "start over" with another representative. 3. They can decide this is a good time to try the competition.

Having only one of your customer-service reps assigned to a customer presents problems for the company as well. What happens when that customer-service rep leaves, and takes with him or her all the knowledge about his or her customer base? What happens to the work load—and the quality of your service—when all the veteran reps are handling more than their share of calls, while new reps are struggling to build new relationships?

What happens when a customer calls with a product question or problem that has to be researched, and the customer-service rep is too busy?

The traditional one-customer-rep relationship can mean operational problems for the company—and poor service for the customer.

Our teamwork approach has solved these problems.

Here's how it works.

Our customer-service department is divided into eight teams of six people each. Each team is assigned to specific accounts.

*The whole team, rather than one individual customer-service rep, builds a relationship with their customers. All six members are responsible for learning as much as they possibly can about the customers they've been assigned.*

We introduce the customer to all members of the team, and give him a special phone number, which will only be answered by someone on their team.

Then from day one, customers call *their* customer-service *team* to place orders. If a team member is sick or leaves, or gets reassigned, there are still five other people on the team who are familiar with the account. They'll know whether the customer always orders mauve or black, or whether they want delivery at the dock or inside. There is no need for customers to start all over again explaining their needs, just because one person leaves.

Plus, with this arrangement, customers get better answers to the questions they have that require research, because there is now someone available to look up what they need. In a traditional customer-service operation, a rep might shun a time-consuming question in favor of a customer with a large order to place. Their incentive might come from the large order, and not from looking up an answer. However, our customer-service rep can afford to take the time to research a product question, or handle a tricky problem, because the sales bonus is based on the productivity of the *entire team*.

And there are other advantages as well. Because our phone system automatically routes a customer's call to the next available member of the customer's team, veteran team members and new employees enjoy a more even work load, and can take time to sell add-on items and build the sales volume in an existing account.[1]

One final note: Before we started our teamwork set-up, the customer-service department had one of the highest employee-turnover rates in the company. The teamwork concept has changed that, and we now have practically no turnover in that department.

---

1. We have almost a one-to-one ratio of sales reps to service reps. If you really want to check the level of service a company can give you, check the number of people they have to service an account, compared to the number of sales reps. If you do, you'll see where their heart is—sales or service. If *you* want to establish a reputation for service, pay attention to these ratios.

## NOT EVERYONE CAN BE ON THE FIELD AT ONCE

> *We need one another.*

Customers get caught up in the team concept as well. They know the name of the team to which their account has been assigned. It could be the Fort Worth Stars, the Dallas Diamonds, the Arlington Top Guns, the Houston Express, or one of the four other teams. (Team members decide on the name, team colors, and they even design a team logo that appears on the shirts they wear.)

And we take the concept of teams one step further. After all, the customer will be dealing with more than our customer-service representatives, if they do business with us. At one time or another they'll be coming in contact with every single aspect of our organization. That's why before customers sign a contract with us, we make sure that they are aware that we believe in teamwork, and make sure we introduce them to representative members of our team.

For proposal presentations in our furniture company, we may take several members of the customer-service team along, plus one of our designers—if the customer is thinking of buying new furniture—and a supervisor from our installation team as well as an accounting rep will also go along. An accounting rep? Sure. Right from the beginning, we want to know what special billing requirements the customer might have.

We want the customer to be comfortable with us. That's why we also give customers the beeper and home phone numbers of our installation supervisors. We encourage them to call these people directly with questions, special needs, or just to get an update on how the work is going. Customers love having that added sense of control—a name, a number, someone to talk to about what's happening.

How do our furniture-installation supervisors feel about giving out their home phone numbers? They love it. They appreciate the confidence we have in them, and they appreciate the opportunity to take accountability for their work. They feel like top management. They feel that they can make things happen—and they can.

What happens if the customer doesn't like a particular team member? We make substitutions. Just like a football coach, project managers may substitute a particular player who relates better to the customer's situation or needs.

However, it does *not* work the other way around. We try to not use temps, or outside contractors—except in emergencies—to supplement our team. Why? People from the outside don't care as much as we do about making our customers happy.

Temporary people, or an outside delivery service, never feel part of your team—they don't even know the salespeople! How are they going to cooperate and help keep promises to customers? What's their investment? Zero.

Customers buy the whole team—both those on and off the field, and they like that arrangement.

Here's an excerpt from a letter we recently received from a new account:

> *We were most impressed with your organization. The tour of your facility provided us an introduction to a well-organized, efficient operation. . . .*
>
> *We were pleased to see the obvious teamwork that was apparent throughout your company. These are the qualities that we recognize as essential to the successful operation of any organization.*

Customers must have confidence in every member of our team, if they are going to do business with us over the long haul. To make sure they stay with us, we constantly strive to develop new players. Let me give you an example of how that works at our furniture company.

Business Interiors teams up their sales reps with an assistant— who really is an apprentice sales rep. If a customer can't reach the sales rep immediately, the assistant is available, and since the assistant is fully informed about what's happening at each step of the sales cycle, he or she should be able to help the customer. We have the same set-up with our designers, and in our accounting department. This way we always have *at least* two people, in *each department,* who are familiar with *each* account.

Customers hate to hear, "That's John's department; you'll have to talk to him about it when he gets back." Our staffing arrangement minimizes the chances of that happening.

Behind-the-scenes people can make the players on the field look successful—or incompetent. That's a message I've carried with me ever since I played football.

When I was playing football, we had a running back who knew how to make everyone work together as a team. When he was successful on a play, he always gave the linemen a tap on the shoulder pads or a "thanks" in the huddle. Although he was a star, he knew that it took eleven players to get the ball down the field.

But things changed after he graduated. The next year a pompous peacock, who didn't care much for team spirit, joined the team as running back. At halftime during one game, we were winning 35–0. He had already scored three touchdowns, and as he sauntered by the offensive linemen, he said, "I wonder what the papers will have to say about *me* tomorrow."

The rest of the team traded glances. About *me?* What about *us?* Since we were ahead, a few of us on the offensive line decided to teach him a lesson about teamwork. At the start of the second half, the first time we had possession of the ball and the quarterback called his number, we deliberately missed making our blocks. He got creamed. On second down, the quarterback called his number again, and again we slipped our blocks. The same thing happened on third down, too. After losing thirteen yards on three straight carries, our new running back got the point. As a team we *never did this again,* and for the rest of the season, he was quick to credit the whole team for his success.

To encourage teamwork anywhere, you have to teach Lone Rangers about teamwork.

## REWARD THE TEAM, NOT JUST THE STAR

> *A team will out-perform a group of individuals every time.*

Equally important, you have to reward the behind-the-scenes people as well as those on the playing field. Salespeople are used to being on a team and competing for expensive awards and trips to exotic places. But we know that the game doesn't turn only on the salespeople's efforts.

After all, it's the support people—the warehouse pullers, truck drivers, order processors, carpet and furniture installers, buyers, and accounting clerks—who deliver on the sales promise. We make sure these people are rewarded too.

For example, the customer-service teams can win awards for any of the following:

- increased productivity
- lowest number of credit returns
- best attendance and punctuality
- highest sales of promotional items.

Warehouse employees win awards based on punctuality and attendance, production, initiative, daily cleanup, and attitude.

Bonuses are shared to encourage team play. When a manufacturer offers a $1.20 bonus for a particular product sold during a special promotion, a portion of that money goes into a "bonus pot" to be divided among all the behind-the-scenes team members who provided support services during the sale.

Traditionally, the salesperson who sold this product would keep the entire bonus. We probably would give 80 cents of that bonus to the salesperson. The remaining 40 cents is split among the support team.

Do salespeople like the support teams sharing the glory and the green? You bet. They understand that they can't do the job alone. In fact, they'll often send thank-you notes, tie balloon greetings to their support-staff chairs, and bring in candy as a way of saying thank you. At least once a year, that thank you is more elaborate. They'll take everyone on their team out to dinner, or to a ballgame. The furniture salespeople gave a turkey to each employee at Christmas. All these gifts come out of their own pockets.

You might have heard the old line, "Nothing happens until someone sells something." Our version goes like this: "When someone sells something, *teamwork makes it happen.*"

## COACH'S CHECKLIST

✔ *Eliminate Lone Rangers.* Have more than one person know the whole story on every project or account.

✔ *Encourage customers to get to know the whole team.* If you do, they won't ask for a specific *person* each time, they'll ask for a *team member.*

✔ *Give out key employees' home numbers.* Customers like it.

✔ *Remind salespeople that teamwork makes it happen.* Make it clear to them that it is more than their wonderful selling ability that closes the sale. Customers are also buying from, and depending on, their support staff.

# 5

# Make Small Customers Feel Big

> *Everyone has an invisible sign hanging from their neck that reads: MAKE ME FEEL IMPORTANT! Never forget this message when working with people.*

WHEN YOU'RE small, you know you're small.

When we bought the business, sales were just fifty thousand dollars a year. Because we were small, many suppliers didn't want to call on us. They would go either to Dallas or Fort Worth. They wouldn't get off the interstate to make a sales call on our small account, which was located halfway in between.

There were a few suppliers, however, who would call on us. Even though they knew we couldn't purchase much, they liked the upbeat, winning attitude we brought to the business. They were on our team through tough and trying times.

There is an old saying, "You dance with the one who brought you." Well, today those loyal suppliers are enjoying our preferred-vendor status, now that we are a $150-million business. The others? Well, they want to be on our team—now. But we'll never forget how they wouldn't take the time to see us when we "weren't big enough." They definitely made us feel small.

What are their chances of making the Miller team? In a word, small.

When a customer is small, he knows he's small. It is your challenge to do something creative to make him feel he's important and that your business couldn't survive without him.

In most businesses—including ours—80 percent of the
comes from 20 percent of the customers. This means you m\
your primary sales team focus on your big customers. But
volume customers should not be neglected. Why? Because:

- They are profitable. Big accounts can demand, and get,
  volume discounts that smaller accounts can't. They just
  don't order enough to justify the reduced price. On
  average, sales we make to smaller customers carry
  higher profit margins.
- They're loyal. Small customers remember who is nice to
  them. We did when we were small.
- Perhaps most important, they can grow.

What do you do to keep the small customers happy and loyal? We
have a tele-serve department that provides personal service to these
customers. We don't send a salesperson out to call on small customers, but we check with them regularly by phone. They're assigned
their own special sales rep, who phones them at a time the customers specify, to make sure they have everything they need, and takes
an order if they don't. As with our large accounts, smaller customers receive free delivery, and monthly usage reports, if they want.

We also send them special catalogs and monthly fliers that list
items of particular interest to small businesses. Because we want
them to have the same educational opportunities our large accounts
enjoy, we invite them to our promotional events and shows.

On the personal side, we want small accounts to know we like
and appreciate them. Here are two quick examples of what we do
for any new account to make sure they know they're important
to us.

First, we send our thank-you-for-buying letter to the secretary or
office manager who places the order. Why? Because those secretaries or administrative assistants routinely get little attention as decision makers, and we want them to know we appreciate their
decision to buy from us. It's important to court the end-user, not
just the president.

On their initial order we also say thanks with a small present.
When the small-volume customer buys from us, or refers other
business to us, we send them a little something they can use around

the office, maybe a paper-clip dispenser, or a letter opener. The expense or size of the gift is not important. Saying thank you, which we also do with a personal note, is.

A buyer's need to feel appreciated is not measured by the size of his or her monthly volume. In corporate America, large accounts often get royal treatment; smaller businesses don't. That's why you'll stand out if you romance the small customer's ego and loyalty. Challenge your team to find cost-effective ways to make small customers feel important. A tele-serve department, a direct-mail service, a "will-call" desk are all places to start, but find other ways as well to make them feel special.

It's funny what happens if you treat customers well. As our small accounts grow, we always ask if they would prefer to have an outside sales rep call on them. But 99 percent prefer to keep the relationship with our tele-serve department intact.

Small accounts are important to us, and they'll remember us as they grow.

## COACH'S CHECKLIST

✓ *Romancing small-volume customers pays off* . . . in higher profit margins and customer loyalty. Don't make small customers feel small.

✓ *Cultivate phone and mail sales.* The cost of sending a salesperson out to visit a small customer can be prohibitively expensive. Look for ways to do business with small-volume customers by phone or direct mail.

✓ *Treat large and small customers with equal concern.* If you are going to thank big customers for their orders, thank smaller customers as well. Just because the customers don't generate huge volume is no reason to ignore them.

**6**

# Make the Lobby a Showplace

> *Customers, vendors, manufacturers, potential*
> *employees, and family members of current*
> *employees all form their first impressions of your*
> *company as they walk through the door into your*
> *building. What kind of impression do they*
> *receive?*

## COMMON COURTESY ISN'T COMMON

ONE OF the most lasting insults to visitors is making them wait. We don't let a visitor sit or stand in our lobby without someone approaching to offer help, directions, or answers. The receptionist will do that the moment he or she sees someone walk through the door. But if he or she is not there, employees passing down the hallway, or through the lobby, will always stop to ask, "How may I help you?"

Common courtesy? In some companies, it's not that common.

When our employees make appointments, they keep them—and at the scheduled time. Vendors and customers get the same treatment when they come to see us; we don't keep them waiting.

Another way to make visitors feel welcome is greeting them personally rather than sending a secretary to escort them to your office. And why should the secretary be the only one to offer coffee or a soft drink? Why shouldn't *you* do it? To visitors, such small gestures speak volumes about the attitude of the employees—and the companies they represent. These personal touches and welcoming gestures convey to visitors their importance to you.

## DOES THE RECEPTIONIST RECEIVE?

> *"She's busier than a one-armed paperhanger with hives, but . . ."*

The receptionist's attitude is no less important. We all can relate to this story.

You have an appointment at noon, and you show up five minutes early. The receptionist, who is on the phone, never glances up as you approach her desk. You wait. The receptionist takes a second call after the first one ends, still not looking up. She takes a third call just as the second ends, this time briefly scowling at you as if to say, "Can't you see I'm busy?"

After the third conversation, she dials a call herself to present a delayed message to another employee. You slip a business card in front of her and glance at your watch. The receptionist ignores both gestures and turns to answer a passing employee, who asked where Tom and Harold have gone for lunch. She picks up a fourth call, still not having acknowledged your presence, and then answers a fifth call.

You're only rescued when the person you're meeting happens to wander out into the hallway, sees you, and motions for you to join him in his office. You receive no acknowledgement from the receptionist when you leave half an hour later.

When was the last time you checked the greeting given by your own receptionist? Are there so many calls coming in that she can't greet visitors? If so, she's not a receptionist; she's a telephone operator sitting in your lobby.

Do receptionists throughout your organization have a genuine smile? Do they chit-chat easily? Can they direct a visitor to the appropriate place? Do they have answers to the most frequently asked questions? Can they give clear directions to other nearby sites—major hotels, restaurants, banks, travel services?

These are all important ingredients in making customers, and all other visitors, feel welcome and appreciated.

If you want to know exactly what kind of job your receptionist is doing, walk out of your building, and head down to the nearest pay phone. Disguise your voice if you have to, call and ask for yourself, or ask the kind of question that you are sure your company receives ten times a day. Then listen to what happens. Does she convey to you the attitude that "she's busier than a one-armed paperhanger with hives"? If she does, you can imagine what your customers think when they receive this treatment.

## MAKE IT THE TAJ MAHAL

How about all the other little things that count? We have a television monitor in our lobby on which we list the names of the day's scheduled visitors—key customers, manufacturers, tour groups. People like to see their names displayed.

What about the small amenities that make a big difference when a visitor is waiting? Do you have a phone in the lobby for their use? Do you have coffee or soft drinks available throughout the day, or current magazines, including the trade publications, for them to browse through while waiting? Are the window coverings adjustable to a visitor's comfort at different times of the day?

Visitors to Hewlett-Packard's customer-education centers love the open refreshment areas where they have free soft drinks and ice machines on a "help-yourself" basis. Colonial Car Wash in Arlington, Texas, invites their customers to stand inside an air-conditioned shelter and enjoy complimentary coffee and tea while they watch the attendants clean their cars. A Dixieland band entertains visitors at Stew Leonard's, a Connecticut supermarket. The Kona Village Resort on Hawaii's big island has a greeter meet you at your car with a glass of fruit punch and a sweet-smelling lei. The Waiohoi Hotel on the island of Kauai not only presents the usual lei, but prints the names of guests on the telephone pads in their room.

These amenities, all little things, convey a strong message to visitors.

At the very least make sure you offer your visitors a clean, well-kept site. Is the lighting outside adequate for their safety when they enter and leave the building? Are the trash cans emptied regularly throughout the day? Cleanliness and attention to the lobby, reception area, and restrooms become the business of all employees in a company that cares about visitors.

And finally, a special note about dealing with vendors. Sometimes vendors feel that they're viewed as a necessary evil, that they're seen as people who constantly interrupt the buyer. Nothing could be further from the truth. Vendors might be bringing news of new products, new services, new industry happenings, or new markets. Because we consider our vendors partners in serving our customers and us, their visits are valued, not a nuisance. If our vendors don't look forward to calling on us, then we're off target. We want them to be part of our team.

### COACH'S CHECKLIST

✔ *Treat business visitors as you would treat a friend who came to call.* Would you keep them waiting? "Forget" to offer them something to drink? Talk on the phone while they are there? Of course not. Treat visitors to your company exactly the same way you would treat a friend.

✔ *Have some fun by putting a visitor's name on a marquee.* Hang paper banners that welcome them. Make people want to visit you. Make them feel they are part of your team.

✔ *Display vendors' names, too.* You want them to be seen as part of your team, and not a necessary evil.

**7**

# Watch for Customers with Muscle Cramps

> *If you are not participating, you are not on the team.*

ON THE field, a muscle cramp can be a warning to get rest or medical attention; unattended, the cramp can put you out of the game. You have to pay attention to your customers' muscle cramps—signs they aren't as happy with your team as they once were. Ignoring a customer's muscle cramp can put you out of business.

Employees have to learn to react to the customer's slightest muscle twinge. Here are some tell-tale signs that something might be wrong:

- An approval signature is now required on their orders, which was never required in the past.
- An unreturned phone call.
- When you ask about future plans, you get "We'll have to wait and see how things go."
- Customers become unavailable to chat when you're in the building.
- You're forced to deal with those farther and farther down the organizational ladder.
- Customers who never solicited bids from competitors now do.

- Customers have competitors' products on site or invite other companies' reps to call on them.
- Customers maintain the status quo for long periods of time, no questions asked.

You can't wait to see if any of these things is an isolated incident. The very first time you sense something is wrong, you must take action. Find out if the customer is in any way unhappy with you or your firm.

## STATUS-QUO CUSTOMERS CAN SURPRISE YOU

Were you surprised by the last item on the list: "Customers maintain the status quo for long periods of time, no questions asked"?

Customers who buy the same things from you year after year sometimes grow restless and wonder, "What am I missing?" "Am I being made aware of the latest products and services?" "Am I using the latest technology?" "Am I getting the best service?" Customers who aren't ordering new products—or at least asking you about them—might suddenly begin to wonder about the greener grass elsewhere. If you don't continually create opportunities to keep these customers informed and up to date, competitors will.

A few years ago, a sales rep stopped by my office. "Coach, I'm afraid I have some bad news. We just lost a good account to a competitor."

"What happened?"

"I don't know," she said.

"You don't know? And they've been a customer for better than fifteen years?"

"Yes, I know, but when I made my call yesterday, the purchasing agent said, 'Starting next week, we're buying from your competitor.' "

I immediately visited the customer to find out the details. The problem, I discovered, was one of attitude. The customer was pleased with our service and competitive pricing, but they had the feeling they were being taken for granted. Our rep had shown up every week with a "What do you need today" attitude, failing to mention new products, services, or systems that we offered. In other words, our rep had become an order taker rather than a salesperson.

While visiting with the customer, I couldn't help noticing a competitive catalog, competitive samples, competitive products. Our salesperson was unaware of these tell-tale signs.

Even quiet, taken-for-granted customers can slip away without fanfare if you're not watching closely for signs of muscle cramps. The secret of dealing with quiet customers—and any of the others that you even suspect might be thinking of leaving—is to talk to them. Ask, "Is there anything wrong?" Most people, like our sales rep, hate to hear that there might be a problem. But you have to know what the customer wants changed, before you can take action.

On numerous occasions when a customer has stopped making purchases or their volume suddenly drops, a driver has stopped and asked, "Is there something that I or our company have done wrong, because I haven't made any deliveries to your company recently." This personal concern is very impressive to the customer. The driver cared. Some drivers aren't as comfortable asking, but if they are aware that the customer has stopped buying or the size of the deliveries has decreased, they pass this information along to the route supervisor, who in turn notifies sales management.

Coach every employee to be alert to any warning signal of customer dissatisfaction. If you don't ask, if you wait until your customers tell you they're ready to leave, it's usually too late to save the account.

## ASK, POINT BLANK

> *A smile costs nothing and is contagious. Your face telegraphs how you feel.*

Ideally, you'll never get to the point where you are worried about your customers leaving you. You will have been in such close contact with them, taking care of them at every turn, that they would never think of giving their business to someone else.

However, if you do sense something is wrong, don't hesitate, and don't beat around the bush. Ask point blank. Say something like, "You haven't had much time to visit with me lately. I'm wondering if we've dropped the ball somewhere." Or, "You didn't stop at our booth at the trade show last month. We missed you. Have we messed up?" or "Your sales volume has been decreasing the past few months. Have I done anything wrong?"

Some companies think they don't have to do this. They say, we guarantee everything we sell, and we give our customers a service number to call, if they ever need help. That should take care of every potential problem.

In the words of the old song, "it ain't necessarily so." To some customers, it's not that you *won't* correct their problem; it's that you've *inconvenienced* them in order to correct the problem.

While you're saying, "Okay, bring the item back, and we'll make it right," the customer is thinking, "Why should I have to go to the trouble?"

That might be the *real* problem, but the only way you'll ever know is to ask.

When my wife Joan and I vacation in Kauai, we frequent the Tidepool Restaurant at the Hyatt Hotel because we appreciate the personal attention and service we receive. On our most recent vacation Joan was sick for several weeks and we didn't go anywhere to eat. Much to my surprise, Ann Weiseman, the manager of the Tidepool Restaurant, phoned my home Sunday afternoon and asked me point blank, "Have we done something wrong? You and Mrs. Miller haven't eaten at our restaurant for the past few weeks." I explained the physical problems Joan was having and that our absence was not a reflection on the restaurant. Needless to say, we ate at the Tidepool Restaurant more often than normal during the balance of our vacation.

One small problem might not break the relationship, but little dissatisfactions add up to real pain over time. It's possible a muscle cramp in one area of the business may cause customers to assume that you perform poorly in other areas as well. And if the cramp is severe enough, it can cause customers to leave you completely.

Here's an example. We caused some customers a severe muscle cramp years ago, when we created a discount office-outlet store. Because our profit margins in this particular store were low, we decided to accept cash only, no credit charges.

After we had been open for a while, our store manager told me that a few customers had grumbled about the cash-only policy. So I called one customer, whom I had known for sometime, and asked him what he thought of our no-charge policy. He was straightforward.

"You know I'd rather buy from you. I love your people. They're friendly and upbeat. But it's not convenient for me to go down to the store with cash all the time. I don't always know exactly what I'm going to buy when I leave my office. I'm not asking you to deliver; I'll carry it out myself. But I would like to be able to charge the things I buy." I told him I would check on this and get back to him. I sent him a letter of apology and a fifty-dollar gift certificate for his time, and for the inconvenience he had suffered. I then called other customers, and a small—but significant—percentage told me the same thing. I did the same for all of them.

The no-charge policy might not have seemed like a big deal to the majority of our customers, but over time more and more might never have returned. If we hadn't asked what the problem was, we would have lost customers and never known why. But we did ask, and we listened to what our customers had to say, and changed our policy to allow them to charge their purchases.

Sometimes customers tell you that their muscles are starting to ache; sometimes they don't. But it's always up to *you* to initiate the communication in order to find out what's going on.

If a customer doesn't feel comfortable telling you what's wrong, contact others in the organization. We always make it a strategy to get to know an entire company so that we have more than one source of information. The more people you know in the customer's organization, the greater your chances for communication if trouble develops.

Early in my selling career with a national business-forms company, I was selling to a large Fortune 500 account. I tried to be friendly and courteous to everyone in the department when I made my sales calls. One day the manager of the department said, "In the future I don't want you to speak with anyone else when you call on me. I am the *boss* of this department." Naively thinking I had no other choice, I followed his instructions. Shortly thereafter he was fired. You guessed it: His replacement changed suppliers because I had stopped being friendly to him. He couldn't have cared less about what I had been instructed to do by his former boss.

From that day on I learned a valuable lesson. I made a point of getting to know everyone at an account, from the janitor or the receptionist to the top management. It takes only a few seconds to say, "Hello, how are you doing?" as you pass their desk or work area. A smile costs neither time nor money.

Ask when you sense that something is wrong. Don't wait until customers defect to your competitor to take responsibility for opening up the communication channels.

Muscle cramps, when left untreated, can pull you off the field. If enough customers experience them, you'll be out of business. However, customers who experience the dull pain of a prolonged muscle cramp can also express undying loyalty to the one who heals them. A customer passionate enough to get angry also has the ability to feel passionately loyal, once you make things right.

## A QUESTION OF ATTITUDE

You can't afford to shrug your shoulders at the idea of customers who "slip away." But you might actually be *encouraging* customers to leave, if you—or people in your organization:

1. have a short-term view of the value of a single customer;
2. see a customer as a number instead of an individual.

Now, either of these two attitudes might not cause the customer to break the relationship with you on the spot, but someone with even mild pain over an extended time eventually seeks relief. And, indeed, the things that cause a customer to leave can be minor.

Let me give you an example of how having either a short-term view of a customer, or seeing a customer as only part of the mass of people who do business with you, can cost you money, and quite possibly your business.

A long-time customer once called to say that he'd been in one of our retail stores, and our employees were "indifferent." I tried to get him to be more specific, but all he said was, "They were cold. They just didn't seem to care. They don't even smile."

I apologized and told him that I was sending him a hundred-dollar gift certificate as my way of saying, "I am sorry for the way you were treated."

"Jim, don't bother, I'll throw it in the trash basket," was his response. "I'm never going to buy from you again."

"Okay, but I'll feel better if I send it anyway."

I wanted that customer back. And two days after he received the gift certificate and a letter of apology, he returned to buy again. But in the meantime, I had done a little checking.

"What happened with Charles yesterday?" I asked the manager of the store that he had complained about.

"Oh, you know him. He's very difficult. . . . he's a pain in the butt. And he never buys much anyway."

"What does that have to do with anything?" I wanted to know.

Obviously the customer was right—the manager needed an attitude adjustment.

"Difficult" doesn't matter. Volume doesn't count. These are short-term views of customer retention that, over time, will take their toll.

When you get a negative signal from a customer, *always, always, always* probe for the rest of the story.


## THEY'RE NOT ONE BIG HEAP OF HUMANITY

Lumping customers into one big heap of humanity dulls sensitivity. Don't let your employees do it. Here's an example. One out of a thousand orders filled wrong equals a 0.001 percent error rate. That sounds pretty good, doesn't it? But to the one customer who got the wrong order, your failure rate wasn't 0.001 percent, it was 100 percent. He or she placed an order, and you got it wrong.

Your front-line people have to learn to see customers individually, not as a steady stream.

Long before Tom Peters made *customer service* a household phrase, I learned about customer retention from a friend of mine who owned ninety-six drive-in dry cleaners.

"Benji, what do you do when a lady comes in and says, 'I brought in five shirts and I got only four back?' "

"I don't hassle her. I give her a gift certificate to a men's store where we have an arrangement for just such situations."

"What if she does it again and again?"

"I keep records on our credits for things like this. If there's a pattern, I'll share my records with her. It's amazing how the complaints from that customer suddenly stop—and she'll continue to do business with us. But if I don't immediately make things right with her when she loses the shirt—or *says* she has lost a shirt—I'm stupid. I can run four-color ads in the newspaper and have sixty-second spots on television promoting my company and its service. But what good does that do me if she plays bridge with three other people that day and tells them we lost her husband's shirt and we didn't make it right? I've lost four people immediately, and all the advertising in the world isn't going to bring them back."

What seemed obvious to Benji isn't obvious to everyone. Take, for example, the guy I bought my nearly bankrupt business from back in 1967. The first weeks in the new store, I was out looking for customers everywhere, and during this time one of my employees told me that the woman I was renting our house from used to be our customer.

Great lead, I told the employee. Since we're renting the house from her, I'll bet she'll be happy to buy her office supplies from us.

"No, she says she'll never set foot in our store again," the employee told me.

"She bought this expensive pen from us and filled it with green ink, because she always signs her name in green. Then she got home, and decided that she didn't like the pen after all. So she brought it back and wanted a replacement. The former owner told her he didn't take back used merchandise."

He lost her forever over a pen! Couldn't he calculate the value of that one customer over a lifetime?

My friend Benji knew early on what situations had potential to give customers muscle cramps. My predecessor, on the other hand, saw only the current month's profit-and-loss statement.

## WATCH THOSE WHO ARE QUIET

You have to coach your front-line people to understand that the most vocal and hostile customers might not be the most dissatisfied. They might not be the ones ready to defect. The ones with the most severe muscle cramps might be quiet, and even apologetic. They might say they feel that they are "bothering you," when they ask you to do something. But if you fail to satisfy them, they'll take their business elsewhere.

They might not say anything at all. Not all customers with muscle cramps let you know about it. We once lost an account because our rep drove up to an automaker's headquarters to take the buyer to lunch in a competitor's car. The buyer never said anything. We only found out after we lost the account.

## COACH'S CHECKLIST

✓ *Ask a customer what's wrong at the very first sign of a muscle cramp.* Always, always, always ask the customer when you sense a problem.

✓ *Get to know everyone on the customer's team.* It helps open the channels of communication and gives you another way to find out if the customer is developing muscle cramps.

✓ *See customers as individuals, not as a group.* It is perfectly all right to want to have hundreds or thousands of customers—but give each individual attention.

## 8

# Keep Your Stats and Pay for Your Errors

> *What affects everyone can best be solved by everyone.*

PLAYERS OCCASIONALLY make errors and disappoint their teammates—the shortstop overthrows first base; the pulling guard misses his block. Despite all your efforts to the contrary, occasionally Murphy's Law will prevail, and you will disappoint your customers.

How you handle those situations gives you another chance to separate yourself from the competition.

## DON'T PROMISE WHAT YOU CAN'T DO

How many times have you experienced a situation where a salesperson has promised you a delivery that you needed, and then failed to live up to the promise? Most times salespeople will say, "Don't worry, I have it under control," when they knew it was impossible to do, but they had your order. Will you buy there again?

On a large furniture installation, we promised the job would be finished in seven days, and the customer was hoping for five days. What we did was offer bonus incentives to our installation teams to get it finished in five days, but we didn't sell the order with a five-day promise. We sold it on a seven-day guarantee. The job was finished when the customer wanted it, in five days, and we paid the bonuses to the teams.

Don't let pride cause you to boast. Never over-promise. Maybe you can produce a miracle, but your customer will perceive it as a failure if you don't do exactly *what* you promise, exactly *when* you promised it. (And if you do pull off the impossible, the customer won't give you any credit. After all, all you did was keep your word.)

## AND IF THERE'S A PROBLEM . . .

Go to the customer with the truth, and tell them what you are up against.

Most people won't do that. They just don't feel comfortable looking a customer straight in the eye and saying, "I made a mistake." But you don't do the volume of business we do without someone, somewhere, making a mistake.

Somebody in the bid process transposes a number. Somebody draws the specs wrong. Somebody ships the wrong merchandise. We're human. Despite checks and balances, despite all the teamwork, sometimes we make a mistake. When that happens, we *always* admit it. Then we fix it.

You never win with elaborate excuses. *Nothing but the truth will do.*

We had a new designer working with a sales rep on a job where we were going to install floor-to-ceiling partitions for a customer. It was a tricky job, and our team wasn't sure what size partition would work best, or what each one would cost. They called the manufacturer's sales rep who told them to put down "the standard nine foot" on the order. The manufacturer meant nine-foot *pricing*. Our sales rep and designer understood the rep to mean "use the standard nine-foot *size* partition. To make matters worse, our team transposed two numbers when it came to writing down the color the customer wanted.

Bottom-line: We delivered panels that were the wrong height *and* the wrong color. Although we could have blamed part of the error on the manufacturer's sales rep—after all, his answer to our questions was ambiguous at best—our policy is truth. We told the customer what we had done.

The customer, of course, didn't give us any medals. But she respected our honesty and let us make amends. We cut the panels down to size and electrostatically painted them on site. Our mistake was costly for us but caused the customer a minimum amount of inconvenience.

The worst mistake we ever made still gives me nightmares. A large client gave us a $2.5-million furniture order and that same month, the sales rep handling that job had the good fortune to land another big order. He got behind on his paperwork and didn't ask for any help.

Looking over the end-of-month Orders in Process Reports, the president of our furniture company, John Sample, knew something was wrong, as the report didn't reflect this large order. He called the rep to see what had happened. It turns out the rep had literally stuck the order for that $2.5-million job in his desk drawer, and he was going to process it when he got caught up with his other orders. He had never placed the order with the manufacturers!

John grabbed the order, stuffed it in his briefcase, drove to the customer's headquarters, and walked in to the vice president's office. "We have not ordered your furniture, which is scheduled to be installed in three weeks. But I intend to do everything humanly possible to get your furniture here on time. I'll understand if you want to take your business elsewhere, but I am more than willing to see personally every manufacturer involved and to appeal to them to meet your deadline."

Reluctantly, the customer allowed us to move ahead. John crisscrossed the United States and visited the president of every manufacturer who would be involved in filling that $2.5-million order and asked for help in meeting our customer's deadline. (With a lot of help from manufacturers, we *were* able to do it.)

The long-term customer relationship is about honesty. *Telling the truth should be your employees' first priority in every situation.*

Most people understand how things can get fouled up in "the system." Our own families and households are laboratories of miscommunications. Obviously, customers want you to do the job right the first time, every time. But when you aren't able to do that, they want to know the *truth*. Even when it hurts. Even when your ego gets bruised. Even if you lose the order.

## SAY YOU'RE SORRY

Some people and organizations have forgotten what effect saying "I'm sorry" can have. Those two words can help you keep a customer who is ready to leave you forever. They can even help you avoid lawsuits. But many times front-line employees seem to do everything in their power to resist saying "I'm sorry." Their attitude: "Accounting or the warehouse screwed up, not me. Why should I take the blame?" Or, they'll say something like, "The customer's being rude; why should I be polite?"

After our first year running the store, Joan and I began to think that there was a chance our little business would survive. So we decided to splurge at an elegant restaurant in Fort Worth. She ordered lobster and I had prime rib. The food was great—except for the rancid butter served with the lobster. We mentioned it to the waitress, who took it to the chef.

A few moments later, she returned with the same container of butter and plopped it back down on our table. "The chef says there's nothing wrong with it."

No apology. No adjustment to the bill . . . just indifference. And we're talking about a couple of tablespoons of butter!

Shortly thereafter, the restaurant went out of business. Evidently, we weren't the only patrons who were treated with an "I don't care" attitude.

Coach your employees to see that they all win or they all lose as a team. They don't get themselves "off the hook" when they make other departments look incompetent. No matter who is at fault, it's important that they apologize.

Customers will like it more if the boss, or a manager, comes over to say they're sorry, too. And if the manager can explain why the mistake happened, and what steps they've taken to make sure it doesn't happen again, it makes more of an impression. But at the very least, customers are entitled to an apology from someone.

An effective apology means that you:

- Listen completely and carefully.
- Say "I'm sorry."
- Explain how the mistake happened, without excusing the error or making others look incompetent.

- State what you can do, *not* what you can't do, about resolving the problem.
- Give a definite time when you'll be in touch again, if you can't solve the problem on the spot.

*Then, after you have done all that, fix the system that allowed the mistake to happen in the first place so it doesn't happen again!*

That, however, is the long-term solution. Short-term, say you're sorry.

Never underestimate the value of sympathy to a customer. We were in such a great mood the night we went out to have our special lobster and prime-rib dinner that we'd have easily overlooked the rancid butter—had *someone* shown concern. Simply saying "I'm sorry" matters a great deal.

## MAKE AMENDS—QUICKLY, CHEERFULLY, APPROPRIATELY

It would be difficult to find a business today that hasn't felt the pressure to improve customer service. You can't check in to a hotel, eat a meal in a restaurant, shop for drapes, or buy a car without finding a card asking "How do you rate our service?" or see somebody wearing a "we care" button on their shirt.

The question is: Do companies really mean it? Can't the hotel tell that the pedals on all its exercise bikes don't work? Can't the restaurant see the toast is burnt? Didn't the drapery shop notice that they had only one designer on the floor while you waited forty-five minutes for a salesperson? Didn't the car dealership realize that you had to complete their paperwork process in a 2 × 2-foot cubicle with only one chair?

The point is that many businesses give lip service to customer service.

They talk about it, but they just don't give it. Otherwise, wouldn't they repair their exercise bikes, serve unburnt toast, have two designers on duty, and find a bigger office with an extra chair? And wouldn't they do all those things *before the customer noticed that there was a problem?*

*Doing* something, not merely *talking about* doing something, sets you apart from the competition.

We recently spent a few nights at a New York hotel free because the hotel believed in paying for their errors. When we had previously stayed there, we were supposed to have an overnight package waiting for us. We were going to deliver the package to our client during our stay. The hotel lost our package and didn't find it until after we left. To try to make amends for causing us so much grief with our client, they invited us to stay with them again, and didn't charge us for our second visit.

When you correct a problem, do it with class—quickly, cheerfully, and appropriately. A poor choice of words can destroy the value of the corrective action.

A grudging apology can be worse than no apology at all. To treat either your customers, or their problems, as insignificant erases any goodwill generated by any adjustments you may make. A positive attitude can quickly turn a negative situation around.

We try to hire people with the right attitude. Obviously, you can tell, to some degree, if someone is a "people person" when you interview them, but we go further. We put everyone we hire through a battery of personality tests, to make sure they will deal well with our customers. Then, after they're hired, we coach them to listen effectively.

## DON'T SET POLICY WITH THE EXCEPTIONS IN MIND

Can people take advantage of you, if your policy is to try to satisfy the customer no matter what? Sure. Should you design your policies to catch the people who might abuse your system of satisfying customers? Absolutely not. In other words, we believe the customer *is* always right, until we find out that they have misled us. Then we let them know.

We discovered that one particular customer's order always came up short. At first, when she called to say something was missing from the order, we just sent the item or items to her immediately at no charge, with no questions asked. But after several more "shortages," we knew something was wrong.

Remembering how Benji—the laundry man—handled situations like this, I drove out to see the customer and discussed the situation. "We seem to have a problem," I said. "Here are all our delivery records and here are your shortages. We have more shortages with your firm than all of our other customers combined. Would you walk me through your process here, so we can find out what's happening?"

"Sure," she said. "Your delivery person sets the order right here in the storeroom. And when I have time, I check it in and put the items on the shelves."

"Could employees drop by the storeroom and help themselves to an item or two without your knowing it?"

"Sure. I guess they could."

We had found her problem. People were "helping themselves," before she'd checked in the merchandise.

We worked with her to improve the check-in system. The biggest thing we did was to shrink-wrap her orders in cellophane. This way she could tell at a glance what was in her order, and at the same time if the cellophane was torn, she knew that people had been helping themselves to supplies.

We would have made a big mistake if we had rewritten our policy to say that *all* customers have to check their orders before our delivery drivers can leave the site. That would have penalized the majority for the dishonesty—or the inefficiency—of a few.

I saw this same principle in action several years ago when we had out-of-town guests who wanted to shop at Neiman-Marcus while they were visiting. While they tried on clothes, I sat down to rest in one of the store's antique chairs. Those of you who know me are already smiling, aren't you? At 6 feet 4 inches and 240 pounds, I'm not exactly a small man. Well, you probably guessed right. The chair broke, and I landed on the floor.

After regaining my composure, I offered to pay for the chair, but the clerk wouldn't hear of it. Her primary concern was to make sure I wasn't hurt. I kept insisting on paying for the chair, and she kept asking if I wanted to see a doctor. The store simply refused to let me pay for breaking their chair. That's class. And that's a far cry from the signs that say: YOU BREAK, YOU PAY.

In general, the customer is always right. And if they're not, help them be right. Quickly, cheerfully, appropriately.

Going beyond what's expected and "right" always impresses

customers, and the friends they tell. If you handle the situation right, 95 percent of your complaining customers will not only do business with you again, but they will be excellent ambassadors for your firm.

## EMPOWER LOWER-LEVEL EMPLOYEES TO CALL PLAYS WHEN YOU HAVE NO TIME-OUTS LEFT

We've found that the faster you correct a problem, the better. The customer wants an immediate adjustment, not to wait for someone to ask a supervisor or "check with accounting."

The best way to create a fast recovery time is to *empower* front-line employees to make customers happy. You have to authorize your front-line people to take corrective action when it's needed.

*Empowering* means that the people who deal with customers have to know when to break the rules, take initiative, and be creative. When they show this kind of thinking, their efforts should be recognized and rewarded, not punished.

Mistakes are inevitable; dissatisfied customers aren't. Unhappy customers, once made happy, become your most loyal customers. Do whatever it takes to turn a negative situation around.

And do it even if the error isn't yours. Those situations in particular create the excellent experiences customers rave about to their friends, family, and colleagues.

Not all companies have discovered the importance of empowerment. At a recent business meeting, our vice president of operations and I had occasion to visit with a management team from one of our largest suppliers. During the discussions, we wanted answers to four very simple questions from the supplier. There was a minimal cost factor to a couple of these questions, and the remaining two questions were really basic. The management team from this Fortune 500 company could not give us an answer to any of our four questions. Their only response was they would have to defer to a higher level of management. Let me assure you that the total financial cost involved in these responses was less than five thousand dollars for the year, and this is a company that enjoys a healthy six-figure annual sales volume with our firm. Their answer was they would get back to us immediately after the top management had reviewed all four questions. Three months later, we finally received answers to our questions.

At this same meeting, their competitors gave us immediate responses, as their management teams had *empowerment.* You can guess whom we prefer to do business with.

The willingness to empower your employees to respond immediately to a customer's needs establishes your company's true commitment to customer service.

### COACH'S CHECKLIST

✓ *Under-promise and over-deliver.* That is the easiest way I know of to satisfy the customer and to make sure that you never have to apologize.

✓ *Say "I'm sorry"—and mean it—if you do have to apologize.* Make amends—quickly, cheerfully, appropriately.

✓ *Empower whenever you can.* Make sure the people who deal with customers can satisfy those customers.

# PART 2

# Innovation: Team Think Tanks Do It First

# Make Happy Customers Happier

> *You become successful by helping others become successful.*

EVEN IF your customer has been happy for a long time, you could be in danger. You just can't take a customer—even a happy customer—for granted. If you let well enough alone, your competitors could be on the customer's doorstep saying that things *aren't* well enough.

Happy customers might not be happy forever. You can never take their current status to the bank. Like spouses, customers can get the seven-year itch. They might begin to wonder, "What else is out there that I haven't heard about? Am I missing something by not looking around?"

Some organizations fear innovation, preferring to hang on to old philosophies like, "If it ain't broke, don't fix it." Or they conclude, "Let's keep doing the things that got us here," expecting no change in the marketplace.

One way a favorite restaurant of mine in Arlington, Marsala Ristorante, surpasses their competition in the area is to consistently offer their customers excellent personalized service and fine dining. Our company not only entertains customers and suppliers, but rewards employees with special luncheons and dinners at Marsala, and we always receive the personalized attention of owners Mike Catoli and Jacob Kohan. Extra touches like a white rose given to Joan on her birthday or special complimentary flaming desserts to delight my two secretaries on Secretary's Day confirm Marsala's commitment to making their happy customers happier.

But even the needs of your happiest customers change as they move through the various stages of business life: growth, maturity, decline, restructuring. Departments change from profit centers to cost centers. The economic, technological, and competitive situations change. You have to change with them.

One way you can be sure you do is by constantly asking: "How can we make our customers happier?" You should do that even if they are already happy.

Here's what I do. When I'm dealing with an account, I always ask, "If I sprinkled you with magic sand, and you could have any extra services you wanted, what other services could I offer you?" You would be surprised at the open and honest suggestions you will receive from that customer.

That may be too corny for you. That's okay. Everybody's different and you have to ask in a way that makes you comfortable. But you have to ask, if you want to hold on to your customers forever.

Customers were happy with our packaging. But we made them happier with shrink-wrapping so they could check their orders before opening them.

Customers were happy with our service, but they are even happier now that we offer to store all their office supplies for them. They can eliminate their stockroom and use us as their stockroom instead.

Customers were happy that we guaranteed delivery of their office supplies within twenty-four hours, but they said they would be happier if they could also get small, noncustom furniture just as fast. We began stocking filing cabinets, desks, and chairs in our warehouse, and guaranteed we would deliver the items to them the next day.

That made the customers happier, but they said they would be happier still if they knew the exact time our furniture delivery trucks would arrive. So our furniture company installed phones in our trucks so our drivers could call ahead with an exact arrival time.

And because we never want to stop making our customers happy, we've taken the idea one step further. We added our Hot Shot emergency delivery service, which allows us to deliver an item shortly after a customer calls.

As you can see, sometimes the innovation comes from customers.

Other times, as in the case of putting phones in our trucks, it comes from an employee at the suggestion of a customer, but either way the result is the same: Happy customers get happier.

## WHERE ELSE CAN YOU MAKE THEM HAPPY?

Sometimes you need to look for ways to make happy customers happier by providing a new product, or a different service.

Business Interiors is a case in point. When we started Business Interiors, we sold and installed office furniture and did corporate design work. But we soon found that our customers had difficulty in coordinating the work we were doing for them with the company that would be installing their carpets at the same time. They needed someone to handle the entire project, so we began to install carpets. We even bought majority ownership in a carpet company to improve the installation service. Once again we made our happy customers happier.

Then we heard customers complain about how difficult it was to find anyone to clean the ceilings and walls before they began a redecorating project. So we began cleaning ceilings and walls.

As time went on, we added electrostatic painting, Scotchgarding, reupholstering of office panels, and general cleaning of carpets, chairs, panels, and tile, because our customers told us it would make them happier.

In 1987, with the Texas economy at a low point, we found happy customers had changing needs. They simply couldn't afford to move to better quarters or buy new furniture. So we expanded our furniture rental division and also beefed up the part of our company that did refurbishing. Among other things, this division upholsters or reupholsters furniture, or the fabric on office dividers.

"How can you make your customers happier?" "What else can you do to make them happy?" Those are two questions that should continually drive a company into new markets and services. Responding to customers' needs is what fuels a company's growth.

Again, when we got into business, we did not offer printing services, but our customers kept telling us they would be happier if we did, so we are now in the printing business. Those customers, and others, kept telling us they liked the fact that we kept adding services that made running their offices easier. But they also told us they would be happiest if we could provide "one-stop" shopping for all their office needs, so we are now looking into offering them advertising specialty items, janitorial and coffee-service supplies. In fact, our new corporate slogan is that we will provide "everything for the office," because we want to keep making our customers happy.

## How Can We Do It Differently?

We want to make our products and services better, but we also want to make our products and services different. Different from the competitor's. And different enough to meet changing needs.

We're not talking about taking major detours—going off into completely new business areas. As you've seen, every new business we've gone into has been a natural add-on to what we were already doing. What we've done is really nothing more than the travel agency offering traveler's checks, or the auto store washing your car after they've sold you a new set of tires. These kinds of things are simple, and easy for you to do as well.

Look for the little innovation that makes a big difference in customer satisfaction. Where will that innovation come from? Your customers might suggest ideas, and sometimes innovation will come from management. But management alone just won't be able to come up with all the innovation required to satisfy your customers. You're also going to need *team think tanks*. Who would be the members of that team?

Managers, of course, but also employees *and customers*.

Employees can provide the fresh perspective and creativity they gain from interacting with customers every day. They work in the "customer lab"—the testing place for new ideas and services. They see ways to do things better, faster, cheaper, and easier, because they're so closely involved in the daily process of pleasing customers. If you are calling on an account every day, as some of our salespeople do or, better yet, have a desk for your sales representatives inside their companies, you're bound to have a pretty good idea of what it is going to take to make your customers happy.

Because that's true, we try to make sure we have as much interaction as possible with our customers. As we've mentioned before, we hold customer focus groups, conduct annual customer surveys, and even send out "report cards," so customers have a chance to work with us as teammates. They get to tell us what we are doing right—and wrong—and what other services they'd like us to perform.

How will you know if you're successful at making customers loyal? Answers to the following questions will give you strong clues:

- Are your customers making repeat purchases?
- Are your customers purchasing new products and new services from you, as well as the products and services that have made them happy in the past?
- Are your customers giving referrals? Referrals represent active loyalty.
- Are the personal relationships between your employees and your customers so strong that your customers would feel as though they're leaving family to go elsewhere?

Negative answers to any of these questions could mean that you are vulnerable to the customer having a "seven-year itch." It also means your innovative spirit is lacking.

We also gather customer data the old-fashioned way—by talking with customers face to face. The presidents of our companies periodically spend half a day with customers, seeking their input: "How are we doing?" "Are you satisfied with our service and products?" "Can we help you in any other way?"

Simply having someone like Mike Miller, president of Miller Business Systems, or John Sample, president of Business Interiors, call on a customer creates tremendous P.R. And while they are there, they are also learning what other services our customers would like us to offer, and what they think about the work we've done for them in the past.

But the visits accomplish two other things as well. First, they can be a selling opportunity. John is particularly good at this. "As long as I'm here," he'll say, "let's talk a bit about your long-range plans. When do you think you'll be expanding that new division? What do you think you'll be needing from us?"

Second, those visits help cement the relationship we have with the customer. Instead of just spending the whole day with the purchasing manager, or whoever it is that buys from us, John or Mike will make it a point to meet the customer's boss. Not because we want to go over the buyer's head—in fact, during those meetings, John and Mike will make it a point to praise the buyer—but just because we want the company president to know how much we appreciate his business. These meetings are another way of tying us closer to the customer. We want people to have a personal relationship with us. We want them to feel bad if they ever decide to switch to another supplier.

And, of course, all the information that Mike and John gather on their visits is relayed to our employee teams, so they can use it to help develop new products and services that can help make our happy customers even happier.

## How Do We Charge the Atmosphere?

But just having an employee team won't lead to innovation, or improved customer service, unless those people work in an environment that encourages new ideas.

How do you do that? Perhaps the most important thing is to keep your team members fresh and creative. Like bread and doughnuts, people get stale in the same job, facing the same routine. So we encourage teams to renew their spirits and perspectives by adding new people to the team, setting up events to encourage mingling with customers at industry functions and interacting with customers who visit our facilities. Teams need a continual rush of new ideas through their veins.

But they are going to be able to maintain that rush only if you allow them to take some risks. If, time after time, management shoots down their ideas, employees will get the message that there is no use even trying to think up something new. You might even be discouraging them in ways you don't know about.

If you really want to know how supportive you are, ask your employees for feedback—and let them be anonymous if they want—about the "risk factor." What do *they* say about their freedom to take risks? The results might surprise you.

It's possible that your employees are reluctant to take risks because they have difficulty making decisions. I tell our people who have that problem to sit down and create a *"Ben Franklin balance sheet."* The way Ben Franklin made difficult decisions was to sit down with a sheet of paper and list all the positive aspects of a decision in one column, and all the negatives in the opposite column. After reviewing all the positives and negatives, it is easier to make an intelligent decision.

This helps, but unfortunately it does not solve the problem. Employees don't have nearly as much difficulty in listing the pros and cons as they have in deciding what the odds should be in order to "go for it."

That's where you—their manager—come in. Should they wait until the balance sheet becomes a 60–40, 70–30, or maybe a 80–20 list? What are your guidelines, and what is your comfort zone for risk? Have you coached and communicated that to your employees?

## COACH'S CHECKLIST

✓ *Ask customers what THEY want.* Recognize that YOU don't define what good customer service is. And neither do I. Only your customers can tell you what good service is. And if you want to know what your customers want, you have to ask them—and give it to them.

✓ *Don't relax even if a customer is happy today . . .* they may not be happy tomorrow. Constantly check with them to see how things are going. In those visits always ask, "What could we do to make you even happier?"

✓ *Let your customers define your business plan.* Add new products and services to meet your customers' needs. Your customers will tell you what new business you should be getting into. The more contact you have with your customers, the more innovative you'll become.

# Identify the Common Interests of All Players in the League

> *Either we're pulling together or we're pulling apart.*

INNOVATION PROMISES rewards for manufacturers, wholesalers, and dealers, as well as for customers. Teamwork can improve the image of an entire industry and increase customer awareness of a product or service. Everybody wins. That's especially true when dealers and manufacturers cooperate.

Dealers and manufacturers don't have to look far to find common interests. Dealers save money when manufacturers do things right. A vendor's mistake costs money and time to correct, and if you are a dealer, as we are, it hurts your reputation. Our customers tend to blame us if the manufacturer ships the product late, or sends the wrong item.

To help improve communications and to cut down on the number of mistakes, we started rating our vendors four years ago. (Our rating form is included on page 87.)

As you can see, we evaluate our manufacturers based on seventeen items, grading them on just about everything we can think of. It's a process we take very seriously. After all, *our* reputation, as well as the manufacturer's, is riding on their service. In order to make sure we get the entire picture of how well our suppliers are doing, we involve all our departments—sales, sales support, operations, purchasing, accounting, and the warehouse—in rating the

## VENDOR QUALITY EVALUATION

| Vendor | | | | | Representative | | Date | | | Overall Performance Score | | | |

| CATEGORY | | 1990 | 1991 | 1992 | +/- | CATEGORY | | 1990 | 1991 | 1992 | +/- |
|---|---|---|---|---|---|---|---|---|---|---|---|
| Management (0-35) Total | | | | | | Purchasing (0-25) Total | | | | | |
| AOPD Support | (5) | | | | | Fill Percentage | (5) | | | | |
| Corporate Responsiveness | (5) | | | | | Lead Time | (5) | | | | |
| Growth Incentive/Rebate | (5) | | | | | Pricing & Contract Program | (5) | | | | |
| Volume Rebate | (10) | | | | | Returns & Policies | (5) | | | | |
| Sales Representative | (10) | | | | | Product Quality & Uniformity | (5) | | | | |
| Marketing (0-10) Total | | | | | | Accounting (0-5) Total | | | | | |
| MBS (Wholesaler) Catalog Representation | (5) | | | | | Receiving (0-10) Total | | | | | |
| Promotional and Advertising Flexibility | (5) | | | | | Shipping Paperwork | (5) | | | | |
| | | | | | | Carton Labeling & Packaging | (5) | | | | |
| Sales (0-15) Total | | | | | | | | | | | |
| Training | (5) | | | | | | | | | | |
| Consumer Work | (5) | | | | | | | | | | |
| Product Samples & Availability | (5) | | | | | | | | | | |

**WEIGHTED OVERALL EVALUATION SCALE**

| 90-100 | OUTSTANDING |
| 80-89 | EXCELLENT |
| 70-79 | AVERAGE |
| 60-69 | MARGINAL |
| Below 60 | UNACCEPTABLE |

NOTE: Numbers in brackets adjacent to each category are maximum ratings for superior performance in the respective category.

**FINAL WEIGHTED SCORE:**

COMMENTS:

manufacturer. We want to know if they ship on time. We want to know if their invoices are correct. We want to know if their packing slips are accurate. We want to know if their products arrive damaged. We want to know how effective their salespeople are. In short, we want to know exactly how good they are.

When we're done, we review our evaluations with the manufacturer. We tell the ones that don't meet our standards what they'll have to do to improve, and we help them if we can. For example, the shipments that came from one manufacturer were consistently damaged in transit. Our warehouse people sat down with them and explained how they could improve their packaging. They did, and now they're one of our best suppliers.

We award the manufacturer who receives the highest rating with our Quality Vendor of the Year plaque during our industry's national convention. Another way we reward our best vendors is to admit them into our Preferred Vendor program. Our preferred vendors have the opportunity to work directly with our sales reps and become a part of our team.

In times past, a manufacturer's rep could walk into any office building in the United States, find a purchasing agent's desk, and say, "I've got a new product for you to try." Or the rep could go desk to desk. No more. With increased security, reps just don't have that option. They need the dealer's sales force to set up appointments to see the customer. We offer our best suppliers—the ones who qualify for our Preferred Vendor program—that access. They go with our salespeople on calls, which not only gives them the opportunity to show customers the new products in their line, but also gives them a chance to learn what customers are buying from their competitors.

On occasion we will also take our furniture customers to our furniture manufacturers' facilities so they can talk to the experts and see, touch, and feel the products. That gives the manufacturers an opportunity to demonstrate their capability, financial strength, and commitment to taking care of the end-user.

Manufacturers need dealers to give them an opportunity to show their products, and we do that another way as well. Once a year, we hold what amounts to an industry trade show for our customers only.

We invite selected manufacturers we do business with to come to Arlington and set up a trade booth at the Arlington Convention Center. Then we ask *all* our customers to come to see the new products and learn more about them. We make it an event! Free food, prizes, games, educational sessions. The arrangement gives our vendors an opportunity to show their wares and get first-hand feedback from customers.

What better way for manufacturers to educate customers on increasing office productivity? What better opportunity for customers to ask manufacturers why they don't make a product that is able to do this or that? Customers gain product knowledge. Manufacturers get a new source of product ideas. Everybody wins.[1]

But the trade show isn't the only place we give our manufacturers an opportunity to learn what the customers want. At the beginning of each year, we sit down with our manufacturers and ask about their goals, expectations, and new products, and tell them what our customers have asked for in the past. Our customers, on occasion, even become pilot sites for testing new products.

The result of all these different programs is simple: We get excellent service from our suppliers, which means we are better able to serve our customers. We do everything we can to try to help our suppliers become successful.

The very idea of letting manufacturers and customers get this close scares some retailers and dealers. Yes, customers can go directly to manufacturers and buy from them, bypassing dealers, and if you're worried about that happening, you might do everything in your power from letting customers and vendors get together. But we look at things differently. We provide our customers with services that they could never get from a manufacturer. Since that's true, we aren't in danger of having our customers going to the manufacturers themselves. Again, we want to help both our customers *and* our manufacturers.

## Solve Each Other's Problems

On the other hand, dealers need manufacturers to make themselves successful. Dealers can order the product, but if the manufacturer doesn't show the reps how to sell it, that product will collect dust on the shelves. If the dealer can't get that product in time to satisfy the customers' needs, or the manufacturer ends up shipping defective merchandise, nobody benefits.

We've become even more creative in teaming up with vendors on specific customer needs and problems. For example, in the past we had a problem when we ordered a name brand of office furniture.

1. We break even on this show. For example, last year we had twenty-seven manufacturers exhibit and as partners with them, we all shared equally in the costs of the show.

It normally took four to five weeks from the time we placed the order for the merchandise to arrive from their factory. After input from several dealers, they agreed to keep their best-selling items in their warehouse in Dallas, and that cut delivery time to three or four days.

The Dallas warehouse helped, but we found we still had a problem. To get the furniture from the warehouse to us, the manufacturer used an outside carrier. Frequently, products were damaged in transit, which created a problem for us and our customers. We had to wait four to five weeks for replacements. So we worked out a solution. We now have our trucks that are out delivering in the area stop at the furniture warehouse and pick up the products. The drivers open the boxes to make sure there's no damage and then deliver the furniture to the customer within forty-eight hours.

Our customers get the fastest possible delivery. We save money and time in ordering replacement parts. The furniture company saves shipping costs. What better example of teamwork?

We feel that we owe our vendors the same loyalty that we give our customers. We, in turn, expect them to be loyal to us and give us their best service at all times.

## Make Peace with Warring Industry Factions

Finally, one of the most obvious places for manufacturers, distributors, dealers, and customers to team up is within their own professional trade organizations. I think this is a wonderful opportunity to unite the industry.

Professional organizations as the hotbed of solidarity? Well, you're right to be skeptical. It doesn't always happen. But it should. Professional organizations can improve the public's perception of an industry. In our case that's certainly true. People used to think of a local corner store, when you mentioned office products. That's no longer the case.

In addition, our trade organization has helped individual members by compiling industry-wide data on sales, earnings, and expenses, which helps each of us figure out how well we are doing compared to the industry average. Specifically, a colleague and I traveled around the country several years ago to conduct seminars for our association members on how to hire the best people and to motivate them to increase productivity and profits.

In the end, manufacturers, distributors, dealers, and customers can win big when they team up.

## COACH'S CHECKLIST

✔ *Reward your best supplier.* Evaluate, identify, and then reward him.

✔ *Make your customers part of the team.* Take them to suppliers; invite them to trade shows that you put on. Make them part of the team. The more you do, the more loyal they'll be.

✔ *Involve everyone*—suppliers, customers, and your employees—in figuring out the best way to satisfy the customer. It should be a team effort.

# PART 3

# Quality: Teams Run the Plays

# Make Quality Specific

> *The difference between success and failure is razor thin.*

A<small>T THE</small> end of a baseball season, do you know how many hits separate a .290 batter from someone who averaged .300? A hundred? Seventy-five? Fifty? No. Just five. The baseball season lasts six months, so all we are talking about is less than *one* extra hit a month.

But what a difference in perception—and salary—that one hit can make. Just one more hit a month can translate into a *huge* salary increase. Just a touch more effort, or skill, can make a huge difference in payoff.

In the 1976 summer Olympics, there were eight finalists in the men's 100-meter race. The gold medal winner beat the eighth-place finisher by less than half a second.

Success is often measured by slim margins and the only time "success" comes before "work" is in the dictionary.

Do you know what your gross revenue would be next year if your salespeople each made one more sale? Do you know how much your earnings would increase if each employee saved just one dollar a week in operating costs? Do you know what your customer-satisfaction ratings would be if each employee solved just one more customer problem?

Service organizations become leaders, not by improving 40 percent in one fell swoop, but by improving forty services by 1 percent today and another 1 percent tomorrow, and the next day, and so on.

Quality is the increased value you offer to customers that gets them to come to you, instead of the competition. It is what also allows you to charge slightly more than your competition.

If quality comes down to doing hundreds of things better than the competition, does that mean quality happens easily? Never. You don't make quality like instant coffee. You don't just announce it, and add water. You don't just go out and buy new equipment and gadgets to automate things.

So how do you gain that slim margin?

## QUALITY IS NOT TANGIBLE

> *Set a goal for yourself. A goal costs nothing.*

Nobody knows what "quality" is—until they experience it. To make quality meaningful, you have to make quality *specific.* You can't just say to employees, "One percent of our customers rated us slow in filling their orders last month." If you do, they'll see customers en masse and pat themselves on the back for pleasing the other 99 percent.

For your employees to focus on the problem, it's better to say, "Fourteen of our customers were disappointed because their orders were late last month. Let's look at what happened with these fourteen customers."

Employees have to think specifically. That's the only way to make quality tangible. Does quality mean averaging thirty-five days on receivables or collecting in forty days? Does quality mean four-hour repair service or six? Does quality mean a customer-satisfaction rating of 9.3 or 9.9? You have to use real numbers and set real goals. Saying "we want to have the highest quality in the industry," without defining what that means, doesn't help anybody. You have to have a goal, an objective, a plan.

To us, quality means thoroughly checking all orders before they go out, even though the people packing our shipments have a 99.8

percent accuracy rate. Quality means delivery within twenty-four hours. Quality means absolutely correct specifications for custom-built furniture. Quality means totally accurate invoicing. Quality means furniture installations without any incident or damage.

You get the idea. Just as coaches meet on Mondays to review the most recent game films and statistics so they can correct problems before the next kickoff, we get specific every Monday morning when we review our performance of the previous week. *Very specific.*

## QUALITY AS A PROCESS

Our biggest challenge was to take our informal approach to teamwork and combine it with our very formal insistence on quality. We were able to do that once we understood that employees closest to the job had the best ideas of what was wrong with our systems and knew how to fix them. Once we understood that, employee involvement in a quality team became part of everyone's job.

Our two largest companies took different approaches to creating quality teams. At Miller Business Systems, they created a QUEST Program (Quality Utilizing Employee Structured Teams) and it has developed into a three-tiered approach over the years. Here is a summary of the three tiers:

1. We started with Process Analysis Teams (PATs). PATs are one-time teams composed of designated members from each department, used to analyze processes within the company. For example, PATs identified and documented the steps we go through to fill an order, such as selling, invoicing, delivering, and so on. We identified ten key steps, or processes, in all.

2. Then we formed thirty-two Employee Involvement Teams (EITs). EITs strive to improve quality within the ten processes identified by the PATs, along with their functional areas of responsibility. Every department in the company has a team and some departments have more than one team because of the number of employees in the department. Every employee is on at least one EIT. In the first year, our thirty-two teams submitted more than two hundred suggestions. Eighty-eight percent of these suggestions

have been implemented to date. To name only a few of the suggestions:

- Our drivers' EIT team, "The Driving Force," totally restructured the driver bonus program, which is working much better for all concerned.
- Our order-processing EIT team, "Magilla's Gorillas," suggested new ways of stocking the split-case section of the warehouse, so that we could get a greater percentage of order pulls in a much more confined area.
- Our administrative EIT team, the "Firefighters," designed a complete recycling program for the company, which in full force should save Millers approximately twenty thousand dollars per year.
- Our purchasing EIT team, "Miller's Money," tracks and publicly displays our daily order-fill percentage, based on customer demand, which graphically illustrates our consistently high accuracy rate of 99.8 percent.
- Our accounts receivable EIT team, "Miller's Mafia," wrote a complete departmental procedure manual on how to process each of their positions, including computer screens. It's now used as the department procedure manual.
- Our account executive EIT teams have designed totally new sales presentation packages for new prospects.

3. If a team's suggestion cuts across a number of departments, or will require more manpower than can be provided by the team itself, a Corrective Action Team (CAT) is formed to implement the idea.

The system—as you've seen—has worked very well. But our commitment to quality doesn't end with these teams. Each individual employee can contribute ideas too. The employees have a feeling of ownership and empowerment. One of our warehouse EIT teams said to a group of visitors one day, "We love the QUEST Program because we get to tell management what to do."

Our QUEST meetings and presentations have been filmed by

CareerTrack, the national training group, and are featured in their worldwide training materials and seminars.

Business Interiors' Opportunities For Improvement (OFI) Quality Program takes a slightly different approach to reach the same goals: "Continuous improvement, Customer satisfaction, Constant cooperation, and Concern or Commitment for employees" (the "Four C's"). Anything that employees think will improve profitability, increase sales, or improve customer relations is submitted on an OFI form. That form goes to the Quality Director, who assigns a team to research possible solutions. The employee submitting the outstanding OFI in each department receives recognition from management, with their photograph in the company publication *BI Focal,* as well as one hundred dollars.

The Quality Process at Business Interiors started with the top management group, which began the Quality Management Team (QMT). The QMT works with the following organizational structure to support the program:

Work Groups. Each department is organized into work groups of ten to fifteen employees. A member from each of these groups is selected as a representative on the President's Focus Group and a member of the Quality Improvement Team (QIT).

QIT. The Quality Improvement Team is responsible for assigning project teams to review and resolve the OFIs and keep the OFI process operating quickly and efficiently.

A remarkable 87 percent of Business Interiors' employees submitted at least one suggestion to the quality program in its first year. In the second year, every single employee contributed at least one idea. Yes, 100 percent employee involvement.

It's interesting how companies look at suggestions. In the United States, companies focus on ideas that either save or make money. Japanese businesses give higher priority to improving the overall management of the company and creating a work environment that employees like.

In Japan, 29 percent of employees offer suggestions to their employers. Of those suggestions, 75 percent are actually implemented. In the United States, one-tenth of 1 percent of employees offer suggestions to their employers. Of those, only 25 percent are actually implemented.

We look at suggestions both ways. We want to make and save

money, or improve procedures, but we also care about our employees' quality of life on the job. As a result, we don't distinguish between ideas that will save us money and those that will improve working conditions.

Once we adopt an idea, we keep the employee who suggested it up to date about what we are doing to implement his or her idea, and exactly how well it is working. Employees like to know how they are changing *their* company.

Although 100 percent employee involvement in a quality program should speak for itself, to have your company QUEST and OFI quality programs recognized worldwide proves the programs work and have merit. Verne Harnish of CareerTrack, which is recognized internationally as experts on quality management, has just released a three-hour film on TQM, the Basics (Total Quality Management, the Basics), which features both Miller Business Systems and Business Interiors. CareerTrack presents world-wide seminars and will be using the TQM series in over 320 cities, from Sydney to Amsterdam.

## MEASURE ACHIEVEMENTS, NOT JUST ACTIVITIES

As a football coach, you can measure how many yards your players gain during a game—how many tackles and fumble recoveries they make, how many passes they throw.

But even more important is how many passes were successfully completed, how many drives ended in a score, and how many times your defense sacked the quarterback. You have to know which statistics to devote the most attention to.

Likewise, we focus on achievements, not activities in and of themselves. Some companies get so bogged down in measuring activities that they lose sight of what those activities represent. They may make poor judgment calls on service in a tight situation, because they are measuring the wrong thing. We try to focus only on measurements that matter.

For example, we don't just measure the number of orders shipped. We consider the key measurement to be *accuracy*. (Our order fill rate is currently 99.8 percent.)

We measure how many customers or prospects actually *attend* our annual product show, not just how many were invited to come. (We want to know what kind of relationship each salesperson has with his or her customers.)

In Customer Service, we measure the *line items* entered by each individual, not just how many calls they took. We measure the credit returns on a particular rep's order, not just the original order. (We want to know if our rep recommends the *right* products to our customers.)

We measure accident-free days for our drivers, not just how many stops they make.

These measurements are all posted visibly in the building for all employees and visitors to see. For example, in our design director's office, we post how many days it has been since someone missed a deadline. We also post the number of orders pulled each day by each order puller. We also post the accuracy rate of orders pulled each day. We post sales volume for the month by product categories. We post our average days on accounts receivable.

We keep quality both *specific* and *visible*.

And we reward our employees for their efforts in helping us achieve our goals. A Business Interiors employee won an all-expense-paid trip for two to Hawaii recently for submitting the most suggestions—ninety-nine—that were implemented in one year. The second-place winner turned in ninety-three ideas.

At Miller Business Systems, entire teams are rewarded for their quality efforts. Every quarter we give the team that has contributed the most to improving quality a paid day off, plus a cash award. The second- and third-place teams receive cash awards.

Winners in both divisions have their names announced over the loudspeaker and receive letters at home from company officers; they are also featured in *Millegram* or *BI Focal,* our in-house newsletters.

We reward both *quality of ideas* and *quantity of ideas.*

## MAKE MEASUREMENTS/STANDARDS
## UNDERSTANDABLE TO EVERYONE

Your measurements don't mean much, even if they are posted and well publicized, if people don't know what they mean.

Our 99.8 percent accuracy rate on filling orders has been our average, but it's important that our employees understand that even it isn't good enough. We're aiming for 100 percent accuracy. Every mistake disappoints a customer. When we evaluate employees—for raises or bonuses—they know what the quality expectations are.

## BUILD THE QUALITY IN; DON'T JUST ADD IT ON

Quality thinking has to begin at the starting line. At the finish line, it's too late to be quality-conscious. Build your quality program from the beginning.

Take, for example, the difficulty we were having in restocking items. We couldn't credit a customer until we restocked the returned item, and that was taking five days. That was too long. Our solution? We became one of the first companies in our industry to adopt bar coding. Now we run the scanner over the item that has been returned, and we know immediately where to restock the item. Plus, that same sweep of the wand generates a credit memo that goes out the same day we get the item back. That's an example of using our computer systems to build the quality in from the beginning.

We built the quality in with our equipment to provide shrink-wrap packaging to enable customers to check their orders immediately; we built quality in with our decision to use our own drivers rather than using contract delivery services; we built quality in with larger labels on our orders so that the customer's internal mail handlers can read addresses more easily and get the right orders to the right desks or departments faster.

Enough about building quality into the *processes*. The more difficult question is: How do you develop a quality *attitude* among employees?

For starters, we make sure that every single employee is part of at least one quality team. Why? Because it underscores our belief that a commitment to quality must come from *every* level of an organization. Our suggestions have an 88 percent implementation rate from the employees, not management. They know that we are responsive to *their* or *our* recommendations. This has gone a long way toward developing a quality *attitude*.

Even our salespeople have been pulled into the quality program. Traditionally, sales reps have focused on the short term, on making the sale today. We encourage them to think about long-term profits and customer loyalty.

What's the most important thing to keeping the customer happy over the long haul? It's never the product. It's always the service.

## PROVIDE QUALITY TREATMENT/FACILITIES FOR EMPLOYEES

If you want your employees to treat customers well, you have to treat your employees well. It's that simple. Employees who feel mistreated at work are not going to go "the extra mile" for the customer.

Quality treatment, in large part, means quality training. We want our people to understand what our goals are, and the best methods for achieving those goals. We didn't hire them because we needed another body. We hired them because they had something to offer our company. By coaching them and giving them the proper training, we prepare them to contribute their best. That helps them enjoy their work more, and it helps us become a better company.

When we have a problem somewhere, we don't lock management away and tell them to figure it out, and then come back and tell everyone what needs to be done. Instead, we sit down with the people involved in the problem and ask them what they think went wrong. Together we analyze the problem and identify what we can learn from it. Then, together, we decide what needs to be done. If you expect answers from employees, they will most likely offer them.

We offer the quality concept as a challenge. It's an approach I borrowed from the late Green Bay Packers coach, Vince Lombardi. During the Lombardi era, any and all teams considered their season a success if they could beat the Packers. "When you're the best, the other teams all set their sights on beating the Packers. When they defeat us, we make their season," Lombardi used to tell his players. "I never want you to make another team's season by losing to them."

Lombardi challenged his team to remain in first place, to be the best at everything they did in life. Likewise, I challenge and coach our team to stay ahead of our competition. From your employees' very first day on the job, you want them to feel like champions. You want them to accept the challenge of staying in first place.

We do that, in part, by communicating with our employees so they understand the reasoning behind company decisions and policies. For example, when we made the decision to pick up unwanted items that cost less than $7.50, we let our people know why. (You'll remember that even though *we* thought we were doing customers a favor by letting them keep the unwanted merchandise free of charge, customers didn't perceive our decision as a benefit. They wanted us to pick up the item and take it back. Even though it costs us money to do so, that's exactly what we do now.) Just by making our employees aware of such business decisions, we're teaching them our *specific* definition of quality—meeting customer expectations.

All our quality goals are specific. We don't say we are going to do the best we can. We say such things as "Punch-free in 'Ninety-three," which is Business Interiors's current slogan. What does that slogan mean?

Once a furniture installation job is completed, a supervisor walks through with a punch list, a piece of paper that lists every single part of the job. If he finds something that wasn't done correctly, he marks that item with a hole punch.

"Punch-free" captures our goal of wanting to be able to walk away from a large installation with no one needing to walk the site to check that everything's been done correctly. That double checking won't be necessary because the work will have been done right the first time. It will be punch-free.

Sometimes we explain the specifics in terms of dollars lost or dollars wasted. For example, I might say, "if we have one employee who is five minutes late every morning, that costs us $x$ dollars. And if we have six hundred employees, and they are all five minutes late every morning, that amounts to $y$ dollars wasted on salary. That waste means we may not have the capital to buy the new equipment some of you want."

When employees learn to see mistakes as dollars wasted, or missed opportunities, they visualize quality in specific terms.

You want your people to understand the true cost of mistakes—in time, money, and damaged customer perceptions.

## EDDIE CANTOR WAS RIGHT

Does the quality quest pay off?

As Eddie Cantor said about the entertainment business, "It takes twenty years to make an overnight success." The payoff usually comes after a great deal of investment in time, work, and money, but it will come.

Our teamwork approach has led to annual savings of over $250,000, a market share growth averaging 7 percent, and an employee turnover rate that has fallen to just 5 percent a year.

But these quality improvements have had more than just a bottom-line impact. Concentrating on quality has increased teamwork, employee empowerment (which leads to higher job satisfaction), and increased customer satisfaction.

The current emphasis on quality in corporate America provides a common national purpose. Think about quality. Rally around it. The team approach to quality is the *most* significant thing we can do to ensure the economic future of America.

### COACH'S CHECKLIST

✔ *Build quality into your process.* Commit resources to quality even when the current bottom line might not support the commitment.

✔ *Make quality a job responsibility for each employee.* Require, review, and reward participation on a quality team.

✔ *Make quality specific.* Tangible. Countable. Define it by hours, dollars, returns, and customer-service ratings. Be specific for every department.

✔ *Spread the word.* Publicize and explain to employees each decision you make that improves quality.

✔ *Measure results and make those results visible.* Display throughout your facilities visual reminders of your progress in your quality program.

# 12

# Develop a Bottom-Up Game Strategy

> *A team without goals is just another ineffective committee.*

P EOPLE WORK hardest to achieve ideas they believe in. And not surprisingly, people have the strongest belief in their own ideas.

A lot of companies overlook that very basic principle when it comes to setting corporate goals. They cloister away senior managers to strategize for the upcoming year, and then have them reappear to tell the rest of the company what it should believe in.

We have a different approach—one that builds ownership and loyalty among *all* our teammates.

At the end of each year, our managers schedule a three-day work retreat away from our facilities to review the past year and to plan a strategy for the upcoming year. But before they go, they make sure they take with them all the information we have gathered during the year from customer and employee surveys, focus-group luncheons, and from our employee-involvement teams.

That, however, is only our starting point. Before they leave, our department managers meet with their employees to solicit further input. What do their people want to accomplish in the coming year? We call it the "wish list." Their goals get as long as a child's list for Santa at Christmas.

These managers, in turn, forward their lists to the company's senior managers and review the lists with them.

Only after they are armed with *all* this information does the top management in our companies go off on the three-day retreat. One of these afternoons is also set aside for physical team-building events outdoors. Planning constitutes the balance of the three-day agenda—based on all the information that they brought with them from our customers and employees.

Here's how it works:

1. *We select a moderator.* The meetings always start on level ground. "Remember that you have no bosses these three days," we remind our people. This is like a sergeant who wants to fight a buck private saying, "I'll take off my stripes and we can step outside." It's not that we intend to argue; our intention is to get quality ideas regardless of where those ideas originate. To make sure that happens, I never moderate these meetings. I don't want my ideas to get any more consideration than anyone else's.

2. *We review the previous year.* We get under way by having all our senior managers give a brief overview of their accomplishments during the past year. This helps set the tempo for the meeting because we are proud of what they've done. However, the focus is the future, not the past. We spend most of our time on *WOTS* and *Wishes.*

3. *We list our WOTS and Wishes.* Managers share their WOTS: Weaknesses, Opportunities, Threats, and Strengths. Again, remember, they are not doing this analysis alone. They are drawing on all the information they have received from their employees and our customers.

The *"Weaknesses"* list tells us where we're not making customers completely happy. Where are we disappointing customers; what service could be better? We also include internal weaknesses—things that make the job unpleasant, more difficult, less productive. Which procedures are slowing things down. No holds are barred during these weakness discussions. We want total candor.

The *"Opportunities"* list includes areas to expand our customer base, plus our geographic markets, our services, and our revenues. Opportunities to cut costs, to use automation or technology.

*"Threats"* include things that might throw a wrench into our efforts, such as an area recession, major new competition, increased costs from suppliers, weak management or employees.

Our *"Strengths"* discussion focuses on what we do well and how we need to improve on our current successes.

Then we move on to everyone's "wish list."

"If money were no object," we ask, "what could we provide to make your job easier? What would allow you to do a better job for the customer? What could we do to make your time at the office more productive?"

Sometimes we can be Santa Claus and come up with the money easily enough. You'd be surprised at the little things that mean a lot. Fixing potholes in the parking lot, providing additional lighting in the warehouse, and adding new wallpaper in the reception area were all little things that made a big difference in morale.

Other "wishes"—such as upgrading the computer system so that we could store more data for our customers—can take a bit longer.

Business Interiors takes a slightly different approach to these planning meetings. First-level employees complete their WOTS and wish lists individually. Without coaching. Without discussion with their supervisors. They just compile a list of what comes to mind.

They hand those lists to their supervisors, who in turn add their comments and recommendations, and pass the expanded list to their bosses. And so it goes up the line.

As a manager, you might have to work hard at getting input from the first-level employee. First, you have to help that employee understand how important his or her ideas are. Then, you must listen to those ideas. The natural tendency is to deal only with people who are one or two levels below you. It is very important to find out what is happening on the bottom rung.

4. *We divide into functional area teams.* After we brainstorm the WOTS and wish lists from all employees, we categorize all the information into areas of responsibility and assign senior managers to lead teams that will prioritize all the suggestions. Every idea is rated either A, B, or C. The As are the *must*-dos; the Bs are the nice-to-dos, and the Cs are the if-there's-time-and-money to-dos. Our teams then begin to formulate plans to achieve these goals during the upcoming year. These teams meet quarterly throughout the year to review the progress they have made on their respective lists.

By following this approach, we've accomplished 98 percent of the A projects and up to 85 percent of the B and C projects over the years.

Just as in coaching, you have to develop a game plan for growth and profits. We've all heard the line, "You can't tell the players without a program." Our version is, "You can't play the game without a plan."

Don't let yourself rationalize away the need to plan by saying things such as: "Our business changes from day to day"; "the marketplace shifts too rapidly"; or "you never know what is going to happen in the economy."

Get a plan. Change it as needs and situations shift, but *get a plan.*

## COMMUNICATE

After the year-end planning session, we communicate our vision to all employees. We put articles in the *Millegram* and the *BI Focal.* The new goals and plans are included in our new-employee orientation. Our company presidents talk to each department to let them know the results of the planning session and the goals for the next twelve months. It is important to let every employee in the company know that his or her idea was heard at the top.

You have to let people know what's going on. Whether you have to rent a civic auditorium, football stadium, movie theater, or a church building to assemble everybody, do it. Firsthand, specific communication from the top has to be a priority. Everyone has to share the vision. They have to see the goal line if they are to cross it. After all, they are part of the team.

Twice each year, the president of each company presents the "state of the company" address, where he meets with all employees in each department, regardless of the shift, and shares with them where we are going, and how they fit into the plan. That address might be formal or informal, ten minutes or an hour, whatever is necessary to ensure that every employee knows what's going on.

Planning and goal setting are not just once-a-year things. Companies must constantly adjust their game plan to meet competitive challenges. Our operating groups meet weekly to make the necessary strategic adjustments.

So what's the result of this bottom-up strategic planning?

Well, one of the first things I learned is that if you ask people to tell you what they think is important, you—the boss—might not always like what you hear. And you might not always get your way.

I remember one of our past think-tank sessions in 1989 in which

I was excited about our "opportunity" to expand into a new market. I was convinced we could really do well if we expanded into San Antonio. I made a great presentation to the management teams, explaining all the pluses and minuses of acquiring an existing company there, convinced we would expand right away. Then we put it to a vote. The result? I was shot down 15 to 1. I think, with a lot of lobbying, I could have gotten a second vote and made it 14–2, but what was the point? We didn't go into the new market. As chairman of the board, I could have rammed the decision down everybody's throat, of course. But if I did, I might win a battle, but I'd have lost the war of employee involvement. Incidentally, we eventually expanded into San Antonio in 1991 with everyone on the team agreeing it was the proper thing to do.

Another situation came even closer to my ego and emotions. My son Mike appeared at my office door one day.

"Dad, you're not going to like what I have to tell you," he began. "But our team thinks we should close our downtown retail store. Now I know that's the flagship store, and the place where you and Mom began the company. But it's just not working. The market in that part of town is gone. It's not in our best interest to keep it open any longer, and I'm the team member that gets to tell you."

The team was right. The market was changing. But that store was my baby. That store was what I paid my life savings, and then some, to buy in 1967. I sat looking at him for a long moment. Then I sadly said, "Well, if that's what the team feels, let's do it. Let's close it."

If you're going to do strategic planning with teams, you have to be committed to what they decide to do. If you're afraid of their decisions, either you've hired the wrong people, or you're not giving them the means to find the right information.

If you ask, *listen*. If you are going to let your people call the plays, let them run with the ball.

## COACH'S CHECKLIST

✓ *Plan from four viewpoints: weaknesses, opportunities, threats, and strengths.*

✓ *Involve everyone in that planning.* Get input from every employee in your company when you set your corporate goals.

✓ *Give teams the responsibility for making their goals happen.* People work hardest on their own ideas.

✓ *Share the vision.* Communicate your final goals and plans so that every member of your team knows the company's objectives.

# 13

# Sell the Best Product or Service and Educate the Customer

> *Asking for help is a strength, not a weakness.*

A DIRECT-MAIL piece for the latest in domestic vacuum cleaners caught my eye a few years ago. "Powered like a tornado, trouble-and maintenance-free, light as a feather," the copy read. All at an introductory, once-in-a-lifetime low price. I bought it.

The thing was light, all right. It felt like a toy, not a tornado—and it performed like one.

Despite the common caveat "let the buyer beware," buyers—including me—sometimes aren't skeptical enough. Customers often fall victim to those who sell them inferior products at low prices.

I'm not just talking about scams and shoddy service or products. It goes beyond that. Customers can simply be taken because they don't know any better. You have to coach your customers about the differences between good, better, and best. Department stores do it all the time. When you shop at a department store, you have the choice of "sportswear" or "better sportswear." You can buy a washer or dryer or you can buy "our best washer and dryer."

When your customers go shopping you need to show (and tell) them you're the best at what you do, and that you offer the best products and service. You can't take for granted that customers will always know quality when they see it.

Our daughter, Kathy, owns and shows Arabian horses. When Joan and I accompany her to a show, we're hard-pressed to pick a winner. That is, unless one entrant looks like it's ready for the glue factory. Yet Kathy and the judges know what a quality horse looks like, walks like, rides like, and shows like.

When it comes to quality, they know and we don't.

Similarly, customers don't always recognize quality when they see it. Unfortunately, it is often too late when they become aware of what's missing.

## DECIDE WHAT YOU CAN TEACH

Our seminars on *ergonomics* (an applied science that coordinates the design of devices, such as chairs, to physical working conditions, such as an office) and carpal-tunnel syndrome (an irritated condition or injury to a wrist membrane that can occur from typing on a keyboard at an improper position) help customers understand the value of proper furniture design. After attending our seminar, they have a better understanding of how their furniture choices can increase the comfort of employees and minimize liability and lawsuits from employee injury.

Our suppliers, such as 3M and Avery, educate our salespeople on product features and benefits and on how to sell these products so that they will benefit the end-user.

Customer education has become a marketing tool for both manufacturers and dealers. You find that art-supply stores teach customers how to paint. Brokerage houses teach financial planning seminars to families and business owners. Real-estate companies teach homeowners how to touch up their houses for resale. Sports shops offer golf lessons for the beginner. Cosmetics companies teach make-up techniques. And so it goes in nearly every industry.

Education, free to the customer, can be the most cost-effective way to spend limited marketing dollars. Ask yourself what can you teach potential customers that will allow them to understand and appreciate your service or product quality. Do your salespeople know how to demonstrate the difference between a leather and synthetic finish? Do the secretaries know your competitors take up to twelve hours to respond to a service call, while you show up in two hours? Do your cashiers know why Brand X costs twice as

much as Brand Y? If your employees don't know quality differences, how can they explain them to customers?

You have to help customers spot the good, better, and best.
Customers will remember quality longer than price. So it's up to
you to coach and educate them about what you offer. That's particularly true with service businesses.

In our business, we're selling service as much as office products.
Our reps sell on-time deliveries. They sell flexibility. They sell accurate billing statements. They sell furniture correctly installed. They
sell monthly usage reports tracked for clients by departments. They
sell the availability of a large inventory for immediate delivery.
They sell access to designers and other technical professionals. They
sell customer training and ease of doing business.

In short, they sell a "no-hassle" experience.

And a no-hassle experience can be worth a lot to customers
these days. But customers can value it only if they know you provide it. You have to coach and educate them about what you
offer.

And before you can educate them, you have to know yourself
*exactly* what makes you different from your competition. Is it your
ability to meet "impossible" deadlines? Error-free service? Technical expertise? Telephone support? What makes your company different from your competitors?

Pinpoint what you are really selling—look beyond just the product itself—*and then coach and educate the customers so that they can
compare you to the competition.*

Even the most experienced buyers can be fooled on occasion.
One of our large corporate buyers accepted and paid for desks that
were imitations of the quality furniture he thought he was buying
from a low bidder. At a glance, the less-expensive desk looked like
the quality desks he had been buying from us; however, the overall
quality left a lot to be desired. The end results were numerous
service calls to repair the look-alikes, and each time he had to pay
for these service calls. Not only did he get inferior merchandise,
by the time he finalized paying for the service calls, he ended up
spending more money than if he had purchased the quality furniture in the first place.

You have to continually coach and educate your customers
about the differences.

## MATCH YOUR LIST TO THE CUSTOMER'S

This entire concept of educating customers about quality assumes that you know what your customers value. You may be offering the best product in the world, and you can tell your customers about it until you are blue in the face, but if the product is not what they need, they still are not going to buy.

Ron Zemke, a customer-service researcher, tells a great story about this in his best-seller *Service America*. While conducting a seminar in a hotel, Zemke decided to do a little experiment about understanding what the customer values. During the morning break, he stepped into the lobby to talk with the hotel catering people about what they thought seminar attendees really wanted in morning coffee service. They told him people wanted quality coffee, well-brewed, served in fine china on a clean, attractively set serving table.

When the attendees returned to their meeting, Zemke asked them what in fact they valued. They said they wanted to be able to move through the service line quickly. They also wanted the refreshments to be located near the restrooms and telephones, so they could take care of other matters quickly and conveniently. *They didn't mention one single thing that the catering staff thought was important.*

The point of the story is clear. If you intend to educate the customer about quality products and services, you have to know how the customer defines quality. More checkout clerks on duty? Someone to carry purchases to the door? More fax lines and toll-free numbers to make it easier for them to reach you? More parking spaces out front? In-house repair staff? Price quotes broken down by region? Lids glued on tighter? Lighter-weight carrying cases? What is it that your customers think is important?

Know what customers value, and then tell them what you offer. The two lists should match; if they don't, you are the one who is going to have to change, not your customers. All the education in the world is not going to make customers buy something that they don't want.

## SPREAD THE WORD

Sometimes the education process is as simple as making your customer aware of the financial stability of your suppliers. Will the manufacturer be around to provide replacement parts or additional products that match? What is the manufacturer's track record? Customers don't always have access to that information, but you do. Pass it along, as part of your education process.

It's up to you to tell customers about the quality you've built in. *You* have to provide the facts. *You* owe your customers that information.

If they don't believe you—and despite all you say they might not at first—then they might have to go to the most expensive teacher—experience.

Recently the cost-versus-price issue hit a customer between the eyes. We had installed furniture for them before, but during an economic crunch, they gave a project to one of our competitors, because their bid on hourly installation was lower. Just a few days into the project, they were calling us for help. "These guys charged us less per hour," the owner said, "but they're taking twice as long as your people to handle the project."

You owe it to your customer to educate them before experience educates them the expensive way. Your customers will benefit, and so will you.

## AVOID THE MUMBO-JUMBO OF "VALUE-ADDED" SERVICES

How do you educate the customer without being obnoxious or without directly knocking a competitor's product or service?

Our solution? We provide customers a checklist of the free services we offer. That way it is easy for them to make head-to-head comparisons with our competition.

On the list we have such things as special catalogs, stockless "just-in-time" inventory, customized computer reports, delivery service, easy returns, technical research and advice, guaranteed accuracy on order fills, and much more. With our comparative checklist, we're sure we will win their business.

Why not have a list like this that features your own strengths? Again, the customer, or prospective customer doesn't know your strengths unless you tell them.

On a sales call, we also point out the distinction between cost and price. If the printers are down for a week because you can't get the toner cartridge you need, what's the cost to your operations? If you need ten more burgundy-colored three-ring binders for your $3.5 million proposal presentation, what will it cost you in the prospect's eyes to postpone your presentation three days, just so you can have the additional binders? These questions cause customers and prospects to reflect on the *true* cost of doing business with someone who might offer a lower price.

Whatever criteria you want your customers to use in their comparison shopping, put it in checklist form. Put it in black and white. Avoid the vague mumbo-jumbo about "value-added" services. *Specifically* list the products and services you offer.

## REMIND THE CUSTOMER TO WATCH

Another facet of customer education is simply reminding customers—daily, weekly, quarterly, annually—who you are, and what you can do for them out on the field.

Buyers and decision makers aren't in the stands for every game we play, so we send them descriptions of what we are doing for them. We send report cards on our past performance—report cards that are based only on the work we've done for them. Those report cards don't include company-wide averages, only how we have performed for them. Customers deserve to know how many of *their* orders were filled accuraely, what percentage of *their* orders were filled completely within twenty-four hours, and so forth.

But we go further. Here's the not-so-subtle sticker we affix to orders:

> Back orders cost you time and money.
> Miller Business Systems saved you both
> with this 100% Filled Order!
> Thank you for your business.

We try to tell customers, without being obnoxious about it, exactly what we are doing for them. We don't want them to take us for granted. It's like a marriage. If you don't tell your spouses you love them, how do they know? They might feel like they are being taken for granted by their partner. We don't ever want our customers to feel that we have taken them for granted.

Special literature educates customers about our recycling program. A catalog of recycled products lets them know we'll pick up recyclable materials, tells them which manufacturers recycle what products, and helps them purchase recycled goods. Most buyers wouldn't know about the recycling possibilities if we didn't bring it to their attention.

Inviting customers to trade shows also educates them about the quality products our manufacturers offer. They learn about new features, ways to increase their productivity, and trends in color and design. And these trade shows, of course, underscore our capabilities as well.

Customers are encouraged to tour our operations—an educational process that lets them see what goes into accurately filling their orders. Industry awards displayed around the building educate them about the kind of service we provide. We send *Millegram* or *BI Focal,* which are published six times a year, to some customers, to let them know about outstanding employees working on their accounts.

We invite our customers to hear speakers talk about what excellent customer service is. For example, we had Ron Zemke speak to seven hundred of the people we do business with. We want our customers to recognize excellent customer service when they see it.

Recently we had Verne Harnish of CareerTrack spend an afternoon with some of our customers, reviewing quality programs and what to expect from a supplier.

Coach your customers in recognizing quality. Don't expect them to "just know it." Be there—with the facts.

This point is brought home in one of my favorite stories. A minister once stood before a large congregation as a guest preacher for the day. He surveyed the crowd in silence and then began, "I'm always a little uncomfortable about preaching to a new congregation. And I'm sure you're a little uncomfortable, too. You're wondering if I'm a good preacher. And I'm wondering if you know what good preaching is."

Do your customers know what good *service* is? Poor service companies hope they don't. Excellent service companies help them find out.

## COACH'S CHECKLIST

✓ *Offer excellent service* and charge accordingly.

✓ *Teach your customers about quality.* Offer seminars and speakers to show prospects and customers how they can benefit from your products and services. Explain to them what makes your products better.

✓ *Help your customers and prospects understand the difference between cost and price.* Give them checklists and worksheets so they can compare what you offer to what is offered by the competition.

✓ *Remind customers what you are doing for them.* Every chance you get. Don't be obnoxious, and don't brag, but make sure they know how well you are performing for them. You don't want them to take you for granted.

## 14

# Hire Quality Employees If You Want Quality Products and Services

> *Hire an A-type person. Hire an achiever. An achiever makes it happen.*

IF YOU plan to offer quality products and services, you need to hire quality people. It's true, you can't make a silk purse out of a sow's ear. Customers can't learn your software program from an unknowledgeable rep. You can't have on-time delivery if your truck drivers don't care when they get to work. The furniture won't "fit right" if your designers can't draw accurate specs. Your customer won't feel loved if your service rep has no empathy.

When you're ready to hire, do whatever it takes to select quality applicants. We administer both aptitude and personality tests to find out not only whether individuals can learn how to do a job, but also to see whether they'll be able to work well with our customers.

We have mandatory drug testing before hiring and we pay a lot of attention to a person's job history. We don't want to hire someone who has had three jobs in five years. We want someone with a stable work background. In addition, we place a lot of emphasis on referrals from our employees. We hire good people, and they tend to have good people as friends.

In short, we are trying to surround ourselves with winners, people who have a "can do/will do/enjoy a challenge" attitude. We will do everything in our power to keep from hiring someone with a "what's in it for me/it can't be done" approach to life.

We are looking for winners, not losers, and the differences are as clear as can be:

### WINNER VS. LOSER

*The winner is part of the answer.*
*The loser is part of the problem.*

*The winner has a program.*
*The loser has an excuse.*

*The winner says, "Let me do it for you."*
*The loser says, "That's not my job."*

*The winner sees an answer in every problem.*
*The loser sees a problem in every answer.*

*The winner sees a green near every sand trap.*
*The loser sees two or three sand traps near every green.*

*The winner says, "It may be difficult, but it's not impossible."*
*The loser says, "It may be possible, but it's difficult."*

*—Anonymous*

## GO AFTER THE SUPERSTARS YOU WANT

If you want superstars, you are going to have to go out and find them. They won't always come walking in the front door.

Frequently, after we've hired a key player from a much larger company, someone from another office-supply company will come to me and say, "I had no idea Harry was looking for a job. If I'd known he was willing to make a change, I sure would have gone after him."

My guess is that Harry, who was earning more than we offered, didn't know he was looking for a change either. Until we asked. Just as in selling, you have to ask for the order. Identify what you have to offer and then make your pitch.

Those with smaller pocketbooks tend to be timid in approaching employees of larger companies, and suspicious when employees from those bigger firms initiate the interview themselves. Don't disqualify yourself from hiring the competition simply because they are the competition. And don't disqualify yourself just because you can't afford to pay them what they are making now.

You may be able to offer exactly what the star player wants—increased authority; the opportunity to make more important decisions; ownership of a complete project from start to finish; bigger opportunity for personal career growth; less red tape; a sense of being an entrepreneur without having to take all the risks.

One caution about superstar hiring: Don't be impulsive. Sometimes people are described as being superstars when they really are not. It's just like drafting college football players to play in the pros. Many times the superstar in college is a bust in the pros. Check things out so that you don't end up with a "can't miss" label that bombs. Mistakes cost money.

For one particular position, we used a headhunter who charged us a huge fee for bringing us a superstar who came with all the right credentials and references. We were starting a new division, to capitalize on new technology, and this person was described to us as *the* foremost authority in the field.

We hired her—with a big salary—and spent forty thousand dollars to buy the "right" inventory she said we needed. It was only after we did all this that we learned she didn't have the social skills to interact with our sales people, and they refused to sell the product, because they couldn't work with her.

Hiring her cost us dearly. Not only were we out the headhunter's fee, the forty thousand in inventory, and her salary until we fired her, but we also lost valuable time in starting that new division.

Don't believe a superstar's press releases until you check out all the facts, references, and past performances.

## HIRE WOMEN AS SALESPEOPLE OR MANAGERS

It's not that men don't have what it takes. We have many talented men in top selling positions, and some are our superstars. But we've learned in our companies that as a general rule, women also do an excellent job as salespeople.

I think there are a lot of reasons for this. Women are often detail-oriented. They're careful to follow up with the customer, to answer all the questions. They handle each account as if it were their own business. When the customer wants something unusual—big or small—they take care of it.

Women are generally attentive and insightful. Consequently, they excel at "reading" customers, and are quick to sense when things aren't quite right. When they do think something might be wrong, they act immediately. They ask questions—in a nonconfrontational way—that uncover the underlying problem. Then they resolve whatever is bothering the customer and make things right. With our largely female sales force—forty-six women and thirty men—customer rapport has never been better and complaints are rare.

Our best women salespeople and executives are organized and are excellent managers of time. With the responsibilities many of them have as wives and mothers, they've learned to put more hours in the day and to use their time effectively. The key is to give them the opportunity to make as much money as their talents allow, tell them what you expect, give them the ball, and get out of their way. Coach them and then trust them to make the right decisions in the field.

Our female employees tend to look at what they've accomplished and then compete against themselves. In that sense, they share the attitude of many Olympic athletes. In training, those athletes are interested in bettering themselves, in addition to out-performing someone else.

Women take great satisfaction in helping others reach their potential. So what if they've finished up their big proposal and are ready to go home for the evening. Another rep needs a couple of extra hands with specs or designs? She'll stay to help her colleague.

We also find that customers receive women well, particularly on cold calls. Women are usually perceived as less intimidating or threatening than men in their sales presentation.

## DRAFT QUALITY PLAYERS FOR YOUR TEAM

> *Hire people as smart as or smarter than you and they will push you to the top.*

As I travel around the country talking to business owners, I'm amazed to find CEOs discussing issues they should have delegated long ago. For example, reviewing all the mail before it is distributed, signing off on minor decisions, signing checks, and much more. When I ask why, their reasons vary: "I can't trust anyone to do it right." "They just don't understand the business (market, industry, economy) well enough." "I can do it better myself." "I don't have time to train them."

The first criterion for hiring new employees should be that they are at least as smart or smarter than you are. Then coach them, challenge them, train them, empower them, tell them your expectations, and get out of their way. These people will push *you* to the top.

## GET YOUR PLAYERS TO RECRUIT OTHER PLAYERS

Quality people want to work around quality people. So they tend to tell their friends and family about a workplace they enjoy. Friends and relatives are our best source of new employees.

Currently, about 35 percent of our new hires come from employee referrals. Like many companies, we pay our people a small bonus (one hundred dollars) when they refer someone we hire who stays with us more than ninety days. Why do we pay the bonus? Because they've contributed to our own profitability with the referral.

## REHIRE THOSE WHO WANT TO REJOIN THE TEAM

Employees who leave and then return can be your biggest disciples. They've discovered that not all companies foster teamwork and a family atmosphere. Rehires send a strong message to other employees that your company is a great place to work.

When employees are thinking, for whatever reason, that they see greener grass somewhere else, we try to catch them while they are in the decision process. If you wait until the exit interview, it's too late; they've already made up their minds. We want to know what we can do to turn the situation around, long before they have typed their letter of resignation.

We won't get into a bidding war to keep people from leaving, but we've found money is not the main issue—even when they say it is. What we will do is tell the employee they are valued, and then we do a selling job to do what we can to keep them in the family and on our team. I explain to them the company is growing, which means there will be opportunities for them in the future. And I tell them loud and clear how much I care about them and respect their work, and I let them know where they could be in the future if they stay with us.

If they decide to stay, everybody wins.

## Don't Short-Circuit Your Checks and Balances

As I've mentioned, we give new employees (whether they work in the warehouse, in sales, customer-service, or management) personality and drug tests—as a check on their judgment skills. But here's the advice I always give our managers: Interview and look at test results. If your judgment and the tests results agree, fine. If your judgment and the tests results don't match, spend a lot more time before you make your decision to hire. Get other people in on the process. In interviewing, more than in any other effort, two heads are better than one. Three or four heads may be the best.

Always check references and records—before you've set your heart on hiring someone. Because the law is putting more and more restrictions on the kind of data former employers can provide, many companies who are asked to provide information on people who used to work for them have concluded the safest thing to do is just to verify dates of employment and job titles. And because of this closed-mouth policy, many prospective employers shrug off the effort of doing background checks.

Don't.

Do whatever it takes to check out references. In the cases where we haven't, we've been sorry. We once hired an applicant who said he used to work for Florida's Forestry Service. When my wife,

Joan, called the number on the résumé, she had difficulty locating anybody who knew him. The more problems she had, the more suspicious she became. After numerous calls to Forestry Departments all over Florida, we discovered he had worked for the Forestry Service all right—as a convict laborer.

Another of our new employees didn't show up for work on a Monday shortly after he was hired. When he'd returned to his apartment after work on Friday, the Feds were waiting with handcuffs. He was wanted for mail fraud.

Don't let an applicant's story deter you from doing your homework. A young man applied for a job, saying he had previously been the owner of a large furniture company. He told us that he sold his business to new owners, who immediately pushed him out of the company. He also said there was no need to check his job history because his only dealings with the new owners was during the buyout, and all the old employees who worked for him were gone. Our supervisor took him at his word, and hired him without checking.

Four months later, after he had created a little suspicion around our company, we belatedly made the reference calls. We learned that our new employee and his mother had stolen a truck and a load of furniture from his former employer. Not only had he never owned the company, he had stolen from it! The *real* owner was relieved to locate his stolen merchandise and truck.

Always check references and job history.

## ADD BENCH STRENGTH

As a manager, you always have to be looking ahead—training the people who are sitting on your bench waiting to play. In a growth period, that's difficult, but always necessary.

Several years ago a warehouse manager came to me with sugar plums dancing in his head. It was time for his annual salary review, and he couldn't wait to tell me about all the things he had accomplished in the past year. He was already counting the raise he was sure he was going to receive.

"I agree with you about your achievements. In fact, there are some additional things that you achieved that you don't have on your list," I said after he had finished making his case. "You've set the world afire this year. I have one question for you, however. Who have you trained to take your place?"

"I don't have anyone."

"Neither do I."

I then reminded him of the previous evaluations I had given him, how we both agreed that he would develop a successor so that he would be more promotable in the future as the company grew, and that there wouldn't be any additional pay *increases* until he had trained a replacement.

"Because you still don't have anyone in mind to take your place, I'm afraid we're going to have to hold off on any increase until you've trained a replacement."

He was shocked. But he began to take me seriously about the need to build bench strength. In fact, the next year, he had two people trained to replace him! All three of these individuals are still with us, and all have had promotions over the years because they developed replacements.

Since that time, we've built in systems for building bench strength everywhere. In our sales areas, for example, junior reps are now teamed with senior reps to learn their accounts. They actually call on the accounts, as well as help with behind-the-scenes research and paperwork. At our furniture company, junior reps get part of the salesperson's commission, and after two years they "graduate" and get their own accounts.

Our approach to training our younger people ensures we won't miss a beat when our senior managers are ready to move further up the ladder.

Bench strength will make the difference in a close game.

It takes quality people to sell quality products and offer quality services. Make sure you have systems in place to hire those people.

## COACH'S CHECKLIST

✓ *Hire people as smart as or smarter than you.* Tell them what you expect and get out of their way. They will push *you* to the top!

✓ *Encourage your team to recruit other players.* Smart, hard-working people tend to have smart, hard-working friends. Encourage them to recruit their friends and pay bonuses for referrals.

✓ *Make "bench strength" a prerequisite for promotions.* Make sure everyone knows they are responsible for training their own replacements.

## 15

# Pay Attention to the Twitch in Your Left Elbow

> *To accept good advice from others is but to increase one's own ability.*

As BABY boomers grow gray, recruiting excellent employees will become tougher and rougher. Why? There simply will be fewer people in the work force. Baby boomers are not having as many children as their parents did, so the employee pool will be smaller.

Yet people, not products, make the difference. Quality has to start with the people who make the products, sell the products, service the products, bill for the products, and deliver the products. They have to be absolutely dedicated to the idea of giving their best. In short, these are the kinds of people we look for.

How do we find them? We have a system. I call it relying on the "twitch in the left elbow." Some say they rely on "gut feelings." They both mean the same thing: that we are relying—to a large degree—on our visceral reaction to the people we interview.

This doesn't mean we don't use all the available tests to predict success in a job. We do. But in large part, all things being equal, the question of offering someone a job usually comes down to something much more personal.

In addition to all the tests, here are some of the things we look at, when deciding to hire someone:

## Appearance

Good grooming is important even for behind-the-scenes people. Some companies think, "They're in the warehouse—what does it matter what they look like?" But in our operation, it matters. First of all, we have customers and prospects visiting our sites and touring our facilities, including the warehouses, on a daily basis.

Second, we feel that dress and grooming can affect employee work performance. If they dress sloppily, they might develop a sloppy attitude about how they do their job. Our employees have a saying, "The order goes to the professional," and that means that not only do they have to do a good job, they should look professional.

And the "professional" approach applies to every single part of our company. "You can't have mud on your feet without leaving tracks on your work performance."

## Body Language

We like to hire people who will hustle, who think quickly, who make decisions quickly.

If they're too laid back, they probably won't make it around our place because we're growing fast. Things change quickly from day to day. We hustle. People don't have to move as if they were on roller skates, but if they *move* too slowly, how fast will they think or work?

What about physical presence? Do they extend their hand when introduced, or wait for the other person to initiate a handshake? Do they smile first? Do they ask questions or wait for yours? We want to know if they'll take initiative with customers.

How about eye contact? We want them to look customers, suppliers, and other employees in the eye.

## Analytical Skills

What would they do if . . . ? Question people you are thinking of hiring about how they would deal with a customer, or a co-worker,

in a specific situation. See how they react. Business Interiors' marketing director has applicants role play, as part of their interview.

Try to catch the people you are interviewing off guard to see how
creatively they think. As I said earlier, if you surround yourself with
people who are as smart or smarter than you are, they're going to
push you to the top.

## TEAM SPIRIT

Has the applicant ever participated on a team—an athletic team, a
fund-raising team, a dorm team? People who have done so understand the give and take necessary to succeed in an environment that
demands teamwork. They have both cooperative and competitive
experience.

But probe a bit deeper. Were they a team leader or always just
a member of the team? How well did they like sinking or swimming
with the team? Did they ever pull anybody out? Did anyone ever
save them? How did they feel about it?

Ideally, the person will have been both a team member *and* a
team captain. We want to hire people who are comfortable leading
as well as following.

## UPBEAT, COURTEOUS, ENTHUSIASTIC ATTITUDE

You can teach skills. You can even, to some degree, teach people
to think. But you can't teach attitude.

If job applicants can't be positive, courteous, and enthusiastic on
the day they're looking for a job, how can they be positive, courteous, and enthusiastic to customers? If you've got someone who's
passive, moody, depressed, and complaining in general, he or she is
going to find it difficult to be cordial to co-workers and customers.
If personal problems are a distraction, employees can't pay real
attention to a customer's needs.

When Kathy White, our daughter and executive vice president at

Business Interiors, interviews people, she makes sure she talks to them at least twice, at different times of the day—early morning and late afternoon. What if the applicant just happens not to be a "morning person"? What are they going to do with customers they have to deal with in the morning?

Knowing whether someone truly has a good attitude is extremely difficult to determine before you've spent an appreciable amount of time with them. And it's a problem all managers and leaders—including ones as great as Vince Lombardi—constantly have to wrestle with.

About two weeks before the NFL draft, Lombardi spoke to the men's club at our church. Afterward I asked him, "Coach, you've got the draft coming up. How do you know who to pick? You've got the team's whole future on the line."

He responded, "Jim, that's a good question. Do you know what we do here at Green Bay? We have the best doctors available in the Midwest. We'll bring in all the blue-chippers before the draft, and examine them from their big toe all the way to the top of their head to find out whether they can play for the Green Bay Packers. We find out how strong they are, and how fast they can run. We know just about everything about them, except one thing."

"What's that?"

"We don't know how much they want to wear the green and gold on Sunday. We don't know if they want to pay the price to be a Green Bay Packer and a champion. We don't know if they have the heart."

Even with all the management and psychological tests available, you just can't measure attitude, passion, and commitment.

However, you can get an idea about those things by looking for specific clues. For example, our design director takes a good look at a prospect's portfolio: How well is it put together? How neat and organized? Do they present it well? Other people look at the way the application is completed: Is it neat? Do applicants pay attention to instructions and detail?

Like many executives who hire people, one of our sales managers asks applicants about their hobbies, but he pays a lot of attention to the answers: "If they're a golfer and they have a four handicap, I know they're not just a weekend golfer. They are playing all the time, which means that they may cut out of work early. If they fish, how often do they go? Do they go by themselves or with their family? How do they know what Lake Granbury is like at eight A.M. when it's raining? Answers to these questions give me a good idea of where their passion is. If they are that committed to their hobbies, it makes you wonder how committed they are going to be to their job."

Sure, we want people to have outside interests. But the question is, what's their work ethic? Does play seem to be more important to them than their work?

The same sales manager also has another excellent twist on the routine interview question: "What are your personal weaknesses?"

He listens, and then asks, "What are you doing to improve in that area?"

The answer to that question tells you about someone's personal drive, ambition, self-discipline, goal-setting. Are they growing? Do they care? Will they commit to getting better?

Do whatever you can ahead of time to try to find out exactly what kind of person you are hiring. And, above all else, don't underestimate the importance of that "twitch in your left elbow."

## COACH'S CHECKLIST

✓ *Hire positive attitude,* along with experience or technical expertise.
✓ *Watch body language as well as appearance.* If you are in a growing company, hire only people with fast body language.
✓ *Look for team experience and team spirit.* Ideally, the person will have been both a team member and a team captain.

# PART 4

# Sales: Teams Turn Up The Volume

# Adopt the Event Strategy

> *A job worth doing is worth doing together.*

MAKE *EVERYTHING* a big deal. That's what the *event strategy* is all about.

Have you ever checked in to a hotel and found someone had arranged to have a basket of fruit waiting in your room? Ever taken a tour of a museum and received a complimentary memento? Ever asked for the check at a restaurant and had the waiter tell you someone else had already paid the tab? You remember those things, don't you? Each one was an event.

Jan Carlson, president of Scandinavian Airlines, talks about "moments of truth"—those times when your customers have an opportunity to form a positive, neutral, or negative impression of you.

We like that concept a lot, but we've taken it a step further. Our *event strategy* says that we should do everything possible to make *every* interaction with a customer a positive one. With each interaction, we want customers to be reminded of why they chose to do business with us.

Most people concerned about quality service have *talked* about "moments of truth," but that's as far as the thinking has gone. There's a vague awareness of the concept in their companies, but nothing more.

What would make the concept meaningful to all employees?

What would make the concept stick in the minds of front-line people every day? Specifics. You have to get specific about how you can give customers a positive impression of your organization each time you deal with them.

This is a concept that the presidents of our two corporations—Mike Miller at Miller Business Systems and John Sample at Business Interiors—have adopted wholeheartedly.

Let me have them tell you a little bit about it, Mike first:

> *When we have an opportunity to do something special for an account, it is a chance to implement our event strategy. Much of our service is routine for our customers; however, we relish opportunities to go above and beyond their expectations.*
>
> *We keep our prices competitive. If we see market prices change, we will lower existing prices to our customers, without their asking.*
>
> *Not only do we have a department dedicated to helping customers find hard-to-find items, we provide technical support so that customers will know the best ways to use them.*
>
> *Going beyond simply taking orders, delivering products accurately and promptly, and billing correctly separates us from our competition.*
>
> *When letters are received from customers or vendors about an employee's outstanding service, "above and beyond" their expectations, we make those occasions an event by publishing the letters in the* Millegram. *The managers also write personal letters to that employee's home, complimenting the employee and expressing gratitude for a job well done.*

That is something that John Sample believes as well. And his people, just like the ones at Miller Business Systems, do everything in their power to make sure every single contact they have with a customer is a positive one. John says:

> *Whenever we have contact with a customer, it is either positive, neutral, or negative. Neutral and negative are not good. If a positive feeling does not result, it is not an event.*
>
> *You can't have positive contact with customers each and every time you interact with them. But you can sure try. The secret is to prepare for those interactions in advance.*

*For example, when we know someone is coming to pick up an item from us, we make sure that there is someone available to load the order or get the product, and help in every way possible.*

*We developed the AIM (Automated Inventory Management) system, a revolutionary asset-management software program, to meet the requirements of major accounts and help them manage their inventory. The AIM system links directly into our computer system and can be provided at the customer's location. To meet the requirements of one account, we also developed an additional bar-code system to track thousands of items in the customer's inventories. We have created a work-order process that also ties into our AIM system.*

*But perhaps the most effective event strategy we have at BI is our "hot line." On a rotating basis, members of our top management wear a beeper and can be reached within fifteen minutes of any call. These twelve managers have decision-making authority. They can make things happen when a customer has an emergency. How you handle their emergencies is something customers definitely remember.*

Every time customers interact with you, they form a judgment about the way you do business. Don't pass up a chance to make another good impression.

Break "moments of truth" into manageable chunks. Then decide what you can do to make these interactions positive. We're not just talking about the absence of trouble. What can you do to make the interaction *positively memorable?*

When a large organization moves from one building to another, or remodels its current space, they have to shuffle a large number of temporarily displaced employees. After we set up a new workstation, we leave a mint on each desk with a note that says, "We hope we've left your workstation in *mint* condition." It's a light touch to call their attention to the fact that we care about the quality of work we do. As a result, they remember us.

Another event occurs when BI furniture drivers make a delivery to a customer. They call from their truck to say: "I'm on my way. What dock should I use this time? Do I need to contact anyone special? Has anything changed since our last delivery?" And if drivers miss seeing their contact person when they make their delivery, they phone again a stop or two later just to ask if everything was okay with the merchandise they left. Along with the furniture and office supplies, they leave behind a positive impression.

When customers come to pick up an order, we make sure they have personal contact with at least one of our employees—whether that means helping them load an order or shaking their hand. That's an event.

On one occasion when someone from a small travel agency walked into our furniture company with a request for a desk and credenza, the salesperson on duty spent extra time and concern for the customer's needs. Not only did the walk-in buy a desk and credenza, they bought seating, carpet, wall treatment, and several other desks and credenzas. The icing on the cake came when their corporate officer then asked us to take care of *all* their agency offices, over one thousand locations throughout the United States. The walk-in request for a desk and credenza has turned into a customer doing over $1 million in volume each year.

After we set up an account with a new manufacturer, we phone to say, "Thanks. We're so happy to be your distributor." We want them to remember the day we became a member of their team.

We carry our *event strategy* into the community as well. In support of our city's Adopt-a-School program, we arrange for students to visit our firm and witness corporate America in action. In addition, as part of a mentor program, we send staff members to area schools to bond with students and counsel them on career moves for their future. Company involvement in community projects is always a very rewarding form of event strategy.

Your own events might include scheduling a dinner to celebrate a contract, making a phone call to a company president to say how pleasant it is to do business with the firm, writing a letter of thanks. Whatever the interaction, find a way to make the customer glad they came in contact with you.

Customers need help in remembering who you are and why they buy from you. Coach your employees to remind them every chance they get.

## COACH'S CHECKLIST

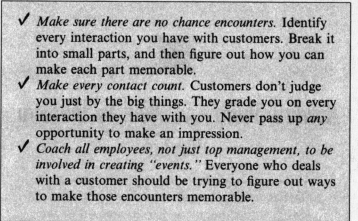

✓ *Make sure there are no chance encounters.* Identify every interaction you have with customers. Break it into small parts, and then figure out how you can make each part memorable.

✓ *Make every contact count.* Customers don't judge you just by the big things. They grade you on every interaction they have with you. Never pass up *any* opportunity to make an impression.

✓ *Coach all employees, not just top management, to be involved in creating "events."* Everyone who deals with a customer should be trying to figure out ways to make those encounters memorable.

# 17

# Reward Teams As Well As the Star Players

> *Eliminate employees who are the "me" type and look for employees who are committed to the "we" principle.*

THERE ARE two kinds of people in the world: those who enter contests and those who don't. If beating the opposition doesn't motivate you, then "helping your team" should. Our teamwork concept appeals to both the cooperative and the competitive spirit.

And we reward both types of people.

In the typical sales organization, only people who compete get rewarded. The top salespeople reap all the recognition and prizes, while the lower performers, and support staff, get nothing. You might want to revamp your sales-commission structure and sales contests to take advantage of the team concept.

If you want star players, reward the stars. If you want star teams, reward team players. We want both—star players and star teams. So, just as on pro teams, our individual players' compensation varies according to their skill and performance on the field, and the whole team gets a reward when they capture our version of the Super Bowl, whether it's achieving a record year or landing a huge account.

Let me tell you how this works, starting with our sales force. We have three types of salespeople: outside sales reps, our in-house customer-service department, and the tele-serve department, which handles orders that come in over the phone. Everybody has a chance to be rewarded as a star player and as a team member.

Individuals earn bonuses based on their personal quotas. And if *everybody* meets their quotas, there is a team bonus. As a result, we have team members encouraging the lower performers and coaching them how to improve.

You get what you reward—star players and star teams.

## PUT YOUR SPIFFS IN A BONUS POT

"Spiffs" is an industry term for the extra commission paid by a manufacturer for selling more of a particular product during a certain time period. Some corporations only give their outside salespeople the spiff money, or give them a percentage of it. The company keeps the rest.

We think that's wrong. We believe spiff money should go directly into the pockets of *all* the people on the team who put forth the effort to sell the product. A big push on a given product takes extra effort on *everybody's* part, particularly those in customer service who say to the customer, "By the way, we've got a special on Product X this month—may I send you a couple of boxes to try?"

Once the item is sold, the warehouse people have to make sure it is packaged correctly and our drivers have to deliver it. The drivers carry extra catalogs describing the promotional item. The catalogs can be given not only to people who have agreed to try the product, but also to those who initially said no.

Since our entire team worked hard to push the product, our entire team should share the spiff money. And they do.

## VARY THE REWARDS

Sure, you want to reward your people for superior performance. But that doesn't mean you always have to give them a check. We've given people free weekends at a local resort; tickets to sporting events or the theater; days off with pay; gasoline paid for the following month or quarter; horseback-riding or skiing lessons; health-club memberships; VCRs; jewelry; baseballs autographed by the Texas Rangers; maid service for six months; subscriptions to magazines or journals; marriage-enrichment seminars; and camp tuition for their kids. We try to be as creative as possible with the rewards.

And one of the things that we always keep in mind is that some people value recognition over riches. Money is soon spent. The trip ends. The lessons are taken, but other forms of recognition—ribbons, engraved plaques or trophies (perhaps presented by a celebrity), letters sent to the family, letters sent to the sales rep's customers or clients informing them that their rep is a winner, articles and photos in the company newsletter—can last forever.

Early in my career, when I was selling business forms for another company, the top salesperson each month got a forty-nine-cent plastic tiger to show he or she was "Tiger of the Month." The salespeople worked like crazy to collect and display those tigers on their desks.

For some, recognition is what it's all about. The hero spotlight warms people for a long time.

## Keep Things Challenging

Figuring out a way of rewarding every member of your team requires some thought. You want to make sure that one person, or one group of people, doesn't win all the time. Otherwise, the contest becomes a *de*-motivator. The fans go home at halftime, and the players wish they could.

How do you keep that from happening? First, you create different goal lines: total sales volume; individual or team quotas; percent of increase over previous records; total volume sold in one product line; account penetration; new accounts opened.

In our customer-service department, part of the rewards program is based on punctuality and attendance. After all, if you're not on the job, you can't take calls for your team. These two areas are part of the criteria used in determining the customer-service team of the month.

Identify what you want to see done and then set up a reward for doing it. You can do this in every department, even accounting. We give out rewards for reducing the number of outstanding days for our accounts receivable.

Our furniture company asks each employee their choice of ways they would like to be recognized, if they are chosen to be rewarded.

To keep competition friendly and challenging for individuals, as well as teams, keep changing what you reward and how you reward it.

## Reward Often

If you drop seventy-five cents in the vending machine, you want your candy. If you win a tennis tournament, you want your trophy today, not tomorrow. Immediate gratification also applies to recognition: Send the letter to your star's customers immediately. Immediately schedule the dinner and presentation. Engrave the plaque today.

If you are trying to sustain sales momentum over a long period of time, plan to reward the salesperson who has shown the biggest year-to-year increase, but consider giving smaller interim rewards, at the end of each month.

## Be Careful About "Out of Sight, Out of Mind"

What good is a name hanging on a plaque in the lobby when customers or vendors coming through the lobby have no idea who it is?

Why not put the trophy, plaque, ribbon, or medal on the workstation of the winning individual? Put it on the winner's briefcase, or post it on the car window or bumper. Place it on the wall as you enter the department that has just won "Team of the Month."

You want an immediate link between name and face. Admiration "from afar" is not nearly as motivating as it is face to face.

## STAND BY YOUR RULES

Once you have established the rules for your contest, be firm. Recently we had a contest where everyone who sold a certain dollar amount of products received a three-day cruise. A top saleswoman missed the trip because she fell twenty-one dollars short. As much as I wanted to, I couldn't let her go on the trip.

If you say everyone who exceeds their previous sales record by 5 percent wins a substantial prize, you can't give out awards if someone is even one dollar short. When the criteria are vague, or depend on the boss's whim, everybody loses.

In one contest we were trying to give bonus money to teams in accounts receivable and accounts payable. But we found performance so difficult to quantify that naming the winning team each month became a judgment call. As a group, the department asked that the program be suspended in favor of a catered lunch for everyone. We agreed.

Credibility—and fairness—demand that contest criteria be clear and firm.

## CHANGE THE LINEUP

Restructure your teams from time to time. Add new hires to different teams. Shuffle the players. Star performers can learn from other star performers. And second-string performers can benefit from watching how different stars do it.

Play off the two things that motivate people: competition and cooperation. Build cooperation among team players while adding competition for fun and challenge. Competition spurs action; cooperation cements the team spirit.

Does it work?

We have a number of star players who earn more than one hundred thousand dollars annually. More power to them! Some companies try to put a cap on a star performer's compensation. That isn't right. Why would you want to take away someone's incentive? Sure, in the *short term,* management benefits, because it is paying out less. But *long-term* management loses, because the employees become disenchanted. Give employees as much as you can.

Low turnover is another indicator that teams work. The turnover rate is exceptionally low within our outside sales force and in our customer-service department. Before we instilled the team concept, everybody wanted out of the "high-stress" customer-service department. Today that department has one of the lowest turnover rates in our company, and we have people waiting to transfer in.

Camaraderie also signals success. Our salespeople reward team members and support teams, such as drivers and warehouse teams, with catered luncheons or tickets to a ball game.

There's competition in the way we structure things, but overall we cooperate. At the end of the game, everybody goes to the dugout saying *we* won.

## COACH'S CHECKLIST

✔ *Design programs to accomplish your objectives.* If you establish a sales quota, or a sales contest, make sure it accomplishes a goal.

✔ *Reward often.* Even if you are holding a year-long contest, establish interim award levels to keep people interested.

✔ *Reward both teams and star individuals.* You need both to win.

✔ *Display scores prominently.* Make the sales race visible. Display plaques, trophies, and commendation letters physically close to the winning individual or team.

✔ *Let people win all they can.* The more they make, the more you make.

# 18

# Put Customers on the Sales Team

> *Teamwork divides the task and doubles the
> success.*

"**W**ILL YOU sell us some furniture?" a caller asked Joan. "I was
at a party last night, and a friend of mine said you and your people
give great service."

"We try, and we'd love to help you, if we can. What is it that you
need?"

"We want to buy some more furniture, but we're getting lousy
service from the dealer we're using. We would rather buy it from
you people."

"And I'd love to sell it to you, but we can't," said Joan, who
proceeded to tell the customer that while we did handle the line of
furniture they wanted, under terms of our agreement with the furniture company, we were only authorized to sell it in Arlington.

But Joan added that even though we weren't the authorized
dealer in the customer's area, she would call the company, and call
the present supplier, to let them know about the service problems
the caller was having.

She did, and the dealership did nothing to improve the service.
The customer phoned us again. And then called a third time.

Finally, the customer said, "Look, I've got furniture to order,
and I want you people to handle it. I refuse to buy from the other
dealership. They don't perform."

When we and the customer explained the situation to the manufacturer, they gave us the okay to make the sale.

Then a second customer called. Same problems with the same local dealer. We tried to help on a number of occasions but nothing happened. This local dealership had forgotten what service meant and ignored their customers. Eventually the furniture manufacturer authorized us to handle that order, too.

The furniture manufacturer then expanded our territory, and our furniture company has now become one of their largest dealers in North America, based on normal dealer net volume.

It happened because customers, who wanted quality service, joined our sales team and opened up a whole new market for us. Customers, as part of your team, make a strong case.

## FIND WALKING BILLBOARDS

Of course, we put customers on our sales team in more traditional ways as well. They send us voluntary testimonial letters that we use in proposal presentations to prospective customers, and they've also taped interview segments in our promotional videos.

Stew Leonard, the owner of the now-famous Connecticut supermarket, has the same enthusiasm going for him when he offers three-dollar gift certificates to any customer who sends him a photo showing the customer holding a Stew Leonard shopping bag near any world-famous landmark. Those attention-getting photos go on a bulletin board. What better investment than three dollars for advertising?

Our customers even demonstrate our products—sometimes with more success than we have. A customer looking through our catalog saw an electronic Rolodex. With these systems, you just hit an initial or two of the person's name and the whole address comes up. The customer remarked in passing, "I'd sure like to have one of those."

So we gave him one. Having demonstrated it to everyone who walked into his office, he has sold over sixty for us so far.

Customers can be your best salespeople if you'll just let them use the product for a while. That's something I learned a long time ago—when I was a customer.

A salesman called on me, when I was a sales manager in Green Bay, Wisconsin. He had this new stapler that he wanted to sell to me, and it looked great.

"Why don't you leave it with me for a few days," I said. "I'll use it, and if I like it, I'll order nineteen, one for everybody in our office."

"Oh, I couldn't do that," the salesman told me. "You'll have to buy it now, if you want to use it."

We were talking about a $5.95 item. I didn't want it free. I just wanted to use it for a week on trial, but the salesman was adamant. As a result, he didn't lose just one sale, but nineteen. If the customers want to try new merchandise, we let them. That way they help us sell the product.

Similarly, we try to get existing customers to mix with prospects at our special events, such as product shows or golf tournaments. A customer bragging about our service beats our salesperson's presentation any day.

On occasion, we join customers in their activities. One thing we especially like to do is work with customers as they plan charity fundraisers. Everybody wins—the charity, the customer heading the fundraiser, and us. Our time is a "thank you" to the customer, as well as another opportunity to have the customer introduce us as "their" furniture company or "their" office-supply firm.

When customers write to say thanks for great service, or to compliment a specific employee for outstanding service, that letter often goes into the *Millegram* or *Bi-Focal.* It's great recognition for the employee, and it underscores for the customers reading the newsletter the high quality of our people.

## DON'T FORGET TO SAY THANK YOU

If customers become part of your team, be sure to thank them.

If you sell software, who are the best salespeople for you? Right—the people at the terminal who brag about how well your software works. Say thank you to them, as well as to their boss.

So often the only person who gets a nice lunch or small thank-you gift is the buyer, the decision maker. Instead, say thanks to all the people who use your products and sing your praises to others in and outside the company.

Cater a lunch for the entire staff. Even cookies and candy go a long way if they're wrapped in appreciation. Make it a mission to let your customers know how much their business means to you. In return, they'll become your best salespeople.

There is one other point I'd like to make about this. You can also generate goodwill, and say thank you for past business, simply by cooperating with customers in tough economic times.

A good customer asked us if they could return inventory for an entire division when they decided to close down that part of their business. We agreed. By taking back their stock and crediting them during a difficult economic time, we earned their loyalty over the long haul. When their situation improved and they reopened that division, guess who recovered that "lost" business, and then some?

### COACH'S CHECKLIST

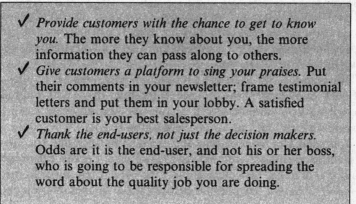

✔ *Provide customers with the chance to get to know you.* The more they know about you, the more information they can pass along to others.

✔ *Give customers a platform to sing your praises.* Put their comments in your newsletter; frame testimonial letters and put them in your lobby. A satisfied customer is your best salesperson.

✔ *Thank the end-users, not just the decision makers.* Odds are it is the end-user, and not his or her boss, who is going to be responsible for spreading the word about the quality job you are doing.

# 19

# Make What-the-Hell Sales Calls

> *You will never know if prospects will buy unless you call on them.*

ROUTINELY, SALESPEOPLE will not make cold prospect calls after 3:00 P.M. They call on existing accounts or just do paperwork and return phone calls until quitting time. If you ask them why they spend their days this way, they're quick to tell you prospects don't buy in the late afternoon.

Nonsense! What have you got to lose if you make a cold sales call after three o'clock? If the prospect is too busy to see you, what have you lost? You weren't selling to this account anyway. I call it a *"what-the-hell" call,* as you have nothing to lose.

John Sample, the president of Business Interiors, had tried to see a facilities manager for weeks without success. Finally, the prospect said, "I've got a two o'clock flight to New York this afternoon. *Maybe* I'll have a few minutes before I leave. Why don't you phone before you come over?"

John had caught our "what-the-hell" attitude. He phoned all the airlines to find out which one had a two o'clock flight to New York. Then he booked a seat across the aisle from the prospect, as a back-up plan, in case his meeting got cancelled, or he needed more time with the prospect. Next, he rented a limo to take him to the prospect's hotel, and had it waiting in case the buyer needed a ride to the airport. What the hell—the guy had to get to the airport somehow.

John walked into the prospect's hotel and called upstairs from the lobby.

"I am here to see you."

"I'm sorry, but I'll be leaving for the airport in a few minutes."

"I'm in the lobby. May I have a few minutes?"

"You're standing in the lobby? Well, sure, come on up."

No sooner had John gotten to his hotel suite and traded pleasantries than the prospect said, "It's been nice meeting you. Maybe we can get together the next time I am in town. But I really do have to catch a cab to the airport."

"No problem. I've got a limo waiting for you outside."

The prospect graciously accepted the ride, and on the trip to the airport, they had an opportunity to discuss all that was necessary to get the account.

This firm is now one of our best customers.

## PRAY FOR RAIN

If you really want to get a prospect's attention after 3:00 P.M., pray for stormy weather, street flooding, or some other natural calamity. Anybody who's out on the streets when everybody else *isn't* makes an impressive showing. Try it and watch the reaction.

What if it's a normal day? What the hell, make a cold sales call anyway after 3:00 P.M. How do you know whether the prospect is happy with their current supplier? Maybe they are ready to place an order with someone new, and here you come with a big smile and—if you're lucky—wet clothes, wet shoes, and wet hair. "Just wanted to touch base with you to see if there is anything we can do to help."

Wouldn't *you* be impressed? We have done it, and it works.

What have you got to lose with persistence? Any time you have a prospect's attention, it's a terrific time to sell.

While making a cold sales call after 3:00 P.M. with a rep we had just hired, I saw a new building from the freeway. "Let's pull in there," I said. It was a perfect day—raining buckets. By the time we got inside, we looked appropriately drenched. The prospect that we cold-called on was so impressed that he offered us hot coffee. We made our presentation, and he placed a small order for some office supplies. I promised next-day delivery.

Impressed with the speedy service, the new customer called the next day and ordered twelve filing cabinets, and he has been buying from us ever since. He spends over a thousand dollars a month with us, years later.

The very next day, the same rookie and I were out again in torrential rain. Again, it was after 3:00 P.M. "Let's make a 'what-the-hell' call in there," I said, pointing to a building I had never been in before, that had hundreds of cars in the parking lot.

She said, "Oh no, not again. Look at my hair."

"Your hair looks fine. Let's go."

The fellow who came out to meet us was someone who went to the same church as my family. I saw him every week, but didn't know what he did, nor did he know what I did. As a result of this cold call, he opened an account and, along the way, three of his children have become our employees. What if we had never made that "what-the-hell" call? Not only would they not be a customer, we would have missed out on three excellent employees.

Remind yourself that after 3:00 P.M., your prospect might actually have more time than at 10:00 A.M. What if that last hour of the day will be the only hour of the month the decision maker is in town? How do you know the current supplier hasn't made a mistake on their order that very day? How do you know the boss hasn't just slammed his fist on the desk and yelled, "Get someone in here who can do something about this situation right now!"

*What the hell, make the call.* Coach your salespeople: "You can always do your paperwork later."

## SAY "THANK YOU" TO REOPEN THE DOOR

But when you do make the call, don't ever take a person's time for granted. Even if the prospect doesn't buy, you've gained an opportunity to follow up with a handwritten thank-you note or letter.

Although many salespeople write thank-you's to those who buy, few take the time to write to the prospects who turn them down. Big mistake! Your thank-you after a turndown always sets you apart from the competition. And of course, it opens the door for a second chance. You can always call again later, to see if that thank-you note arrived. And that second call gives you another chance at selling the prospect.

One final point about making "what-the-hell" calls. Don't make them early in the day. If the prospect gives you a hard time on the cold call, that can destroy your attitude for the whole day.

After 3:00 P.M., though, you don't run that risk. If the call goes badly, you can just go back to the office and catch up on your paperwork.

Make the call. What the hell have you got to lose?

## COACH'S CHECKLIST

✔ *Keep playing until the whistle blows.* Consider 3:00 P.M. to 5:00 P.M. prime time for making cold calls. You can always do your paperwork later.

✔ *Use bad weather as an impressive door-opener.* The fact that you are willing to go out and ask for a prospect's business, when everyone else is warm and dry indoors, will set you apart from the competition.

✔ *Thank prospects for their time.* Send them thank-you notes or letters, even if they didn't buy from you. Then call to see if the letter got there. That follow-up call gives you a second chance at making the sale.

# PART 5

# Problem-Solving: Teams Find Solutions

# 20

# Tell the Players Your Problems

> *People support what they help create.*

A FEW years ago some of the comments we heard from our employees on their opinion survey were like this one: "Our insurance costs have skyrocketed. We need to find ways to get better coverage at a lower price." As a result, we challenged a team of eighteen employees chosen from several departments to review our insurance program and come up with an answer.

They did. Unfortunately for me, their timing was a bit off. Just weeks before I was scheduled to have surgery, the team decided we should go with a new HMO plan. My surgeon, a friend who had been treating me for eighteen years, wasn't a member of this HMO. That meant the insurance company wouldn't pay for my surgery.

In order to qualify for payment, I would have had to change doctors.

Did I have second thoughts about delegating the insurance problem to employees? Yes.

Did I change their decision? No.

Commitment to teamwork won out over personal inconvenience.

Teamwork for problem-solving means compromising your control, and unleashing the unlimited creativity of your employees to come up with solutions. The new HMO plan offered strong financial incentives and allowed employees to choose between using a doctor or hospital that was part of the HMO network or a physician or hospital that was outside the HMO network and pay the additional cost of that choice. Seventy percent of our employees participated in the plan.

Employees will come up with solutions, if you let them.

## CHOOSE UP SIDES

In our experience with teamwork, we'd say there's not much motivated teams can't do. Here are some of the other problems we've presented to our employees:

*How do we coordinate the interoffice delivery of mail and office supplies when our four companies are physically separated?* Do we have to hire new people to deliver mail and supplies between locations? That, of course, is one solution, but the money we spend there won't be available for other projects.

The employees' solution? Company drivers, who pick up merchandise at all four locations, will take our mail and office supplies along with them.

*How do we keep "rental" furniture from disappearing?* When a customer doesn't place their order soon enough, we rent them what they need. We take a chair, or whatever they need, out of stock and rent it to them. Two months later if they need to rent another chair, nobody knows what happened to that first chair. How can we keep better track of all this furniture?

The employees developed a new system. All our rental furniture is now bar-coded, and we can tell at a touch of a button where every piece is.

*What is "perfect attendance" for purposes of calculating team awards?* If somebody attends work every day, except the day his grandmother died, does he still have perfect attendance, or does taking the day off for the funeral ruin it for him and for the team? What kind of policy do you want to have for figuring out who should receive a perfect-attendance bonus?

Our employees defined the guidelines. You now are credited for attending work if you attend a funeral for a member of your family.

*How do we lay out the warehouse to make it more efficient?* Before we moved, we wanted to know how to design the new warehouse. Where did we want the docks? What kind of seals work best around the dock doors? Where did we want the vending machines?

The employees came back with a layout, well within deadline, and created an order flow pattern that gets the merchandise out to our customers faster.

*How do we get our returned merchandise back into stock faster?* When our drivers return to the building, they used to unload the things our customers had returned and put them on our catch-all shelving. It sometimes took up to five days to do the paperwork to return items to stock and credit the customer.

Our employees came up with the idea of using the bar-code wand not only to track the location of the merchandise, but to generate a return slip as well.

These are just a few examples of how employees can help solve company problems. If you empower and communicate with them about problem areas and situations, they will help solve them for you.

## SUGGESTIONS DON'T JUST HAPPEN—COACHES MAKE THEM HAPPEN

To make a suggestion program successful, you have to stay with it. Employees need to know that you're not going to criticize their ideas, and that in fact you'll respond to them. That takes time. People will be hesitant to make suggestions at first. They'll be afraid to stick their necks out, or they'll think that you really don't want them to come up with ways to spend your money. That's natural. But if you keep encouraging them, and responding to their suggestions, eventually everyone will become a bit braver, and before you know it, employee involvement will become part of the way you do business.

The benchmark for such programs has to be Toyota. In 1951, about 8 percent of their employees submitted 789 ideas. Twenty-three percent were adopted. In 1955, 10 percent of their employees submitted 1,089 suggestions and 43 percent were adopted. In 1965, 30 percent of their employees submitted 15,968 ideas, of which 39 percent were adopted. In 1988, 95 percent of their employees submitted 2.6 million ideas—96 percent were implemented.[1]

Patience pays off. Good ideas need time to grow.

And what if there are some things you don't want them to decide? That's okay too, as long as you're up front with them about it. If you're considering a major acquisition, a new capital investment, you might not want to turn that decision over to your team. That won't be a problem—*as long as you make it clear why this is something you would rather leave to management.*

Also, be sure to let employees implement their own ideas. At some companies, management grabs an employee's idea, and then jumps in to devise and implement a solution or plan. It's far more effective to let the team that came up with the idea figure out the how-to's as well. They'll take ownership. You'll get their commitment. And you'll also get more great ideas from these teams in the future.

Finally, management must abide by the decisions the teams come up with, if they make sense. I learned that lesson first-hand when our marketing people decided to close my flagship retail store.

Patience. Clear challenges. Putting the responsibility for implementation in the hands of the idea-generators. Commitment to move with the results. That's what it takes for teams to work.

1. Yuzo Yasuda, *40 Years, 20 Million Ideas* (Cambridge, MA: Productivity Press, 1991).

## COACH'S CHECKLIST

✓ *Share your challenges with your employees.* Let them know about the problems you are facing, give them all the facts they'll need to ask the right questions, and let them come up with solutions.

✓ *Take employees' solutions to problems seriously.* If you can't implement it, tell them why, in detail.

✓ *Let the people who come up with a solution implement it.* The entire program will work better if employees are able to translate their ideas into action.

# 21

# Let Them Have Their Say, If Not Always Their Way

> *Make employees feel like part of your family and part of your team.*

ANGRY PEOPLE will have their say. They have to. If they don't, they'll explode. They'll tell everybody else in their department about the problem. Or worse, they'll tell every customer they come in contact with. Or they'll sabotage the efforts of others, or wreak havoc with their own assignments.

By providing people with a method of talking back, you diffuse hostility that might be building to an explosion. Our employees might not always get their way, but they always have their say. Good and bad. Our suggestion programs, departmental meetings, employee involvement teams, bottom-up strategic planning, and annual employee surveys are all formal attempts to understand what our employees value and what they dislike.

## GET THE FACTS

If you don't have formal feedback channels, don't kid yourself by saying, "But our employees know we have an open-door policy." A general invitation to make an appointment with the CEO sounds meaningless to lower-level employees, and they'll rarely take you up on it without further nudging. Why? Because they are afraid to.

*Everyone* knows that you don't tell top management anything they don't want to hear.

You know that isn't so, and I know that isn't so, but most employees don't. That means an invitation "to have your say" has to be more actively extended—and that's exactly what John Sample does at Business Interiors.

When we first created our quality process, John decided he wanted to get feedback and accurate information from every area of the company. He scheduled meetings, and invited nonsupervisory people from every department. Much as Noah did for his ark, John asked two installers, two drivers, two designers, two accounting clerks, and two receiving clerks to serve as his sounding board.

With this panel in place, John began asking questions. "What are the barriers to making your job easier?" "What decisions would you like to make if given the authority and opportunity?" "What responsibility would you or your group like to have?" "Where are we wasting the most time?" "What is the most complicated form you use?" "What would you like to see changed?"

As one who already managed by "walking around," John was amazed by what he hadn't heard while wandering through the warehouse, or standing on the dock. He was told:

"We want to have regular meetings." The company now has monthly meetings.

"What is the direction of the company?" The company now holds group meetings and publishes the *BI Focal*, which keeps employees informed about the company.

"Only the president or vice presidents make decisions." Decisions at lower levels are now made at that level. John and the vice presidents don't make these decisions.

"There isn't enough training." Job and task training were initiated.

"A vendor is shipping damaged product." Meetings were held with that vendor and vendor tracking was initiated.

"Reviews are late and inconsistent." A follow-up system was established for completing reviews in a timely manner.

"Departments are not cooperating together." Interdepartmental meetings and problem-solving efforts were initiated.

Six months later he repeated the entire process. Dismissing that first committee, he pulled together a second, and later a third, and fourth, and he kept going until he felt he had heard the whole story

166    PROBLEM-SOLVING: TEAMS FIND SOLUTIONS

about what was going on at Business Interiors and had heard it
from the bottom up. By this point, John knew he had gotten the
unfiltered, unvarnished truth. As a result of the subsequent queries,
further refinements were made to the initial employee requests. For
example:

The company meetings that were established organized departments into teams with their own mission statement.

The request for information about the company's direction was
carried to the annual planning meeting where the "bottom-up"
strategy (which will be discussed later) was used to gather employee
input.

The complaint regarding officers and upper management making
all the decisions brought about the review of quality suggestions
and implementation at the lowest levels.

The request for additional training has been enhanced by adding
*front-line leadership and personal training* for all managers.

He also uncovered additional requests for change. For example:

"There is favoritism among the departments and personnel."
Peer evaluations and additional employee surveys were initiated.

"Safety is not checked enough." The company added a safety
committee, and random drug testing.

"Incorrect information is being received about our budget status." Corporate meetings were added with teams discussing where
the company is in relation to budgets.

John still continues to seek information by making sure that he
goes to lunch at least once a month with randomly selected employees. Because he is sincere in wanting input, they are up front
with him.

If you have never gone after internal information so relentlessly,
try it. I guarantee you'll be totally amazed. It's not that supervisors
and managers don't tell the truth; it's just that they see things
differently from the people they manage. They might overlook the
unpleasant, or highlight the atypical.

Remember looking through a kaleidoscope as a kid? That's what
it's like viewing your company from the top level only. At each level
of the organizational ladder there might be a slight distortion in the
information being relayed. The higher up you go, the more dis-
torted the view. Whether it's intentional or unintentional, the result
is the same: inaccurate information. A communication gap.

No matter what your management position might be, you have to *work* to get all the facts that people have turned into conclusions. If you do, you'll find that some of the conclusions were valid, some not.

Rather than encourage employees to keep their mouths shut, we want them to tell us what is truly going on. We don't want employees to feel as though they have to make their feelings known vicariously. We want to know what *they* think and how *they* feel, and we want to hear about it first-hand.

Sometimes employees just need to tell us that they need a better tool to do their job. For example, in accounts payable, people said, "We spend too much time writing down the same information over and over again. If we could just create a fill-in-the-blank form, and be able to cross-reference those notes by customer, we would save a lot of time."

So we sat them down with someone from data-processing, and together they created a software program that did exactly what they wanted.

Here's another example of how employee involvement made us more efficient: Every time we find that an order has been filled incorrectly, we correct it, of course, and then we go back to see what went wrong. Too often employees told us the problem was in the way we had laid out the warehouse. "You've got all the staplers right next to each other," they said. "It's too easy to grab the wrong color or brand."

So we redesigned the warehouse, separating like objects. Accuracy rose dramatically. What appeared to be an "order-puller" problem was actually an operational problem. We fixed the system, and performance improved.

## GIVE MANAGERS AN ''IDEA SWAP''

Managers also need to have their say, and they need to know that someone, or some group, will actually listen to them. Just about every week we have interdepartmental meetings so that managers can have their say, and swap advice. These meetings can be a "show and tell," but they're more often an "ask and act." The issues that come up can vary from motivating a poor performer to developing new training programs. Here are the sorts of things you'll hear our managers say:

"I've got Joe, who's still not responding to our quotas. Here's what's happening. Does anyone have any suggestions of what I might try with him?"

"We've had two different vendors offer sales training to our people, and the programs are not working. Does anyone have suggestions of other programs we might look at? What are you doing about sales training in *your* department?"

Your managers need a way to let off steam and seek advice from other experienced managers about persistent problems. In some companies, going to the boss, or someone else on the same level, is an admission of weakness. In ours, it's considered a show of strength.

## THE BIG ESSAY

Just in case the informal channels of communication don't work for some people who want their say, we conduct an annual employee opinion survey.

Our last question says, "Please use the space below for any comments—either positive or negative—you would like to make about any aspect of the organization, your job, your supervisor, etc."

We give everyone a full page for their expressions, and we expect them to open up and give us their comments.

For this to work, you have to assure everyone of confidentially. We have an outside market research firm administer the questionnaire and compile the responses. We never see the originals.

The anonymity provides employees with the freedom to give honest feedback that we could never get if we did the survey ourselves.

## WATCH THE "YEAH, BUTS"

It's one thing to listen, it's quite another to do something about what you've heard. Give employees a formal response to your surveys. Let them know exactly what you are doing in response to their comments.

This accomplishes two things. First, if they talk, they want to know you've listened. Second, they might see that the only thing they dislike about the company is what the majority of their peers say they value most. They'll become more aware that what pleases them might not please someone else. A report card puts things in perspective—for everybody.

In the process of doing this, watch the tendency to "yeah, but" your way through the comments. You know—"that's a real good idea, but we can't do it because . . ." If the status quo is better, so be it. But be careful that you don't find yourself just going through the motions.

You'll frequently get great suggestions if you ask employees for their ideas. For example, our team approach to quality can be traced back directly to our employee surveys. The employees told us they wanted to be included in the decision-making process, and they also said they wanted to open up communication between departments, and so the idea of quality teams was born.

Other ideas we've gotten? Well, we created a 401(k) benefit plan, started a recycling program, implemented a drug policy, and upgraded our computer system, just to mention a few, all because we asked employees for solutions to difficulties we were having.

This is not to say that employees only want their say when it comes to solving problems. They also like to comment on positive things—growth, new ventures, hiring additional staff.

Here's an example of that. We invited our employees to compete with a firm we hired to design a new corporate logo for Miller Business Systems. We ended up going with an employee's design. The employee, who worked in our design department, won a trip for two to Cancun for coming up with the winning logo.

You'll be amazed with the amount of management time you'll free up if you let employees get involved with the problems you're facing. Not only will they help you solve the problems, they will also gain a feeling of being team players on your team.

Management wrestled for months with a driver-incentive program, but couldn't come up with a win-win solution for all the parties involved. Mike Miller turned this project over to the drivers themselves, who came up with a plan that called for paying bonuses that increased *geometrically* for people who continue to drive safely over long periods of time. The plan also called for the drivers to be rewarded for perfect attendance, and for coming to work on time every day. We thought these were good proposals and we adopted them. Since the programs were established, accidents have decreased, and tardiness and absenteeism have been reduced dramatically. *Their* program is working like a Swiss watch!

Several years ago, our marketing manager came to us with an expansion idea—a discount office-outlet store. We mulled it over. With discount outlets for everything from groceries to electronics, why not office products? The entire management team thought it was a good idea and worth trying. This retail store featured discontinued products, surplus stock, special buys, close-outs, and used furniture.

In the end, the store didn't work. Still, our investment in teaching risk-taking paid off handsomely for many other projects down the line.

For example, in a down economy we acquired three existing office-supply companies in markets where we previously had no distribution. In each case the results have more than justified taking the risks, despite the economic conditions at the time.

With the Texas economy still suffering in 1991 and 1992, we expanded our total operations from 337,000 to 430,000 square feet. Not only did we expand our facilities, our overhead expenses also increased.

Our operations department wanted to streamline the way we picked customer orders, and the expansion into the new Miller Business Systems facility provided that department with the opportunity to pioneer a carousel system for processing orders. This recommendation of our vice president of operations required an initial investment of over six hundred thousand dollars, but it enabled us to improve our efficiency for our customers.

Employees have to be given the freedom to have their say—positive or negative—to feel a part of the team.

What are the limits of letting employees have their say? We don't know yet. The more "say" you give them, the more you'll learn.

When you give people the freedom and confidence to tell you what they don't like, they also tell you what they do like. One of our survey questions says, "List three things that you value most about this company." The responses varied. ". . . I really enjoy working at Miller Business Systems. As a front-line manager I am allowed the flexibility to run my department without my supervisor or upper management watching every move. I really appreciate the freedom." ". . . without a doubt, this is equally an employee-driven and customer-driven company, with more support, recognition, and encouragement from management than I have ever seen or known of . . ." ". . . I especially enjoy working for a company of integrity, whose reputation is flawless in the community. I am proud that this company feels supportive and responsible toward its employees . . ." "I enjoy the team approach, the family atmosphere, and working for a company that emphasizes quality and customer service. . . ."

You need that feedback as well as any negative comments your employees want to make. Once you identify what employees value, you'll know what carrot to use in recruiting. You'll know where to spend your money when it comes to employee benefits and incentives. In short, you'll know what to do more and less of.

Find ways for employees to have a say in the positive changes—growth opportunities, fun decisions, and high-visibility ideas. Also give them a chance to tell you what they think should be changed. But remind them, "You can have your say, but not always your way."

As long as you really listen to what they have to say, everyone will benefit.

## COACH'S CHECKLIST

✓ *Set up systems for employees to tell you what they really think.* Find out what's truly on your employees' minds.

✓ *Ask employees what they value, as well as what they don't.* Positive feedback will help you decide where you should be putting your resources.

✓ *Make sure you get accurate information on surveys.* Include open-ended "essay" questions on employee surveys, guarantee confidentiality, and put together informal feedback teams from the nonsupervisory staff.

✓ *Respond to employees' suggestions.* Listening is not enough. You also have to act. Let employees know what you are doing in response to their ideas.

# PART 6

# Employee Loyalty: Teams Feel Like Family

# Avoid Light-Switch Thinking

> *"Be yourself.*
> *You can be anything you want to be with the*
> *talent that God gave you."*

EARLY IN my career, while I was working as a sales rep for a large forms company, my boss asked me to take a psychological test to see whether I was suited for management. The results showed, among other things, that challenges, not money, motivated me and that I could be a successful manager.

My boss might not have been the motivator to inspire me, but he sure knew how to read the test results. Shortly after he got my scores back, he scheduled a meeting for the two of us at corporate headquarters.

"You've passed the management tests and we've got a new challenge for you."

Excited, I asked, "What is the assignment?"

"We want you to revive a four-state sales area for us, recruit your sales team, and expand our efforts there. We want you to capture this market for us."

"Great."

"You've done well as a sales representative for us in Milwaukee. We've got seven hundred salespeople, and although you are a relative newcomer, you are one of the top ten producers. But then a lot of people can sell. Very few salespeople can manage. If you can manage, *you will be twice as valuable to us.* We want to see what your real potential is. . . . The salary is $14,500, plus a chance to earn bonuses that could give you another four thousand."

This was in early 1963. In 1962, I made $43,000 in commissions as a sales representative. But by the time the boss got through telling me what a great challenge this was, I felt that he was doing me a favor by paying me $14,500.

My first sales job in my new position was persuading my wife that I hadn't lost my mind in wanting to trade a secure territory and comfortable income, sell our new home, and relocate with three small children for a downtrodden district and take a $28,500 pay cut for this privilege.

I told Joan there would be rewards down the line. After all, my boss had promised if I produced. Promotions. Increased responsibilities. Salary and bonuses commensurate with my performance on the new turf.

We moved to Green Bay, from Milwaukee, and I began putting my sales team together. Within four years, the sales office was one of the company's top producers, not only in increased sales, but also in profits.

My boss and I had scheduled a time to meet in his office in Des Moines, Iowa, to review the team's performance at the end of that fourth year. Knowing he was a stickler for statistics, I put together a presentation that would wow a mathematician. With dozens of charts and graphs that showed exactly how successful our team had been, I confidently walked into his office ready to collect on all the financial promises he'd made.

"Just great," he said when I was done. "You're doing a terrific job in Green Bay — you are five years ahead of our projections." He went on for some time, praising me and my team for our accomplishment.

"Thanks for the vote of confidence," I said when he was through. "Let's talk money?"

"No."

No?

No. To everything. He suddenly had amnesia.

I showed my exasperation, and started to remind him of everything we had talked about four years before, that if I could manage I would be *twice as valuable to the company.* He jumped up from his chair and stomped over to the light switch. He flipped it off and on several times.

"Jim, that's what you are—overhead—just like the lights. Sure, your team has had four great years, but every day when you go to work in Green Bay, you cost us money. There's the office we have to rent, the secretaries' salaries, travel expenses, in addition to the other expenses we have to pay. When you were a straight commissioned salesman in Milwaukee, you made money for us. Now you *cost* us money."

That day made an indelible impression on me about respect for employees, the importance of an employee's self-esteem, and about why you must keep your promises if you're a manager.

It doesn't take anything as dramatic as flicking a light switch to make employees feel unimportant. Just an unreturned hello will do.

Periodically, back at that same job, I used to teach sales training at corporate headquarters. Each morning when I was teaching, I ate breakfast in the dining room, and I'd see the company president there reading his *Wall Street Journal.*

Every morning it went exactly the same.

"Good morning, sir. How are you?"

There was never an acknowledgment. No smile. No nod. Nothing. Granted, he might not have known my name, but what would it cost for him to smile, or nod, or simply say, "Good morning"?

How long has it been since you've stopped to consider how much power you have to make or break an employee's day? As one American Airlines employee remarked recently, "When [Chairman] Bob Crandall sneezes, the whole company—one hundred thousand employees—catches a cold." Every boss has that effect on the employees.

You can make them shake or make them smile. Remember their name, smile, and say *"Terrific"* when they ask, "How are you?"

It's the little things that quickly fester and destroy an employee's self-esteem on the job. Reserved parking only for the senior executives. Plush executive suites for the VPs, while lower-level employees sit on rickety stools. Sequestered dining rooms for the executives; vending machines for the rest. Think about how those differences make people feel.

## GIVE THEM MORE THAN A TIPTOE HOLD

Another even more shattering blow to self-esteem is an employee's tiptoe hold on his or her own job. I'm referring to putting employees in the position of having to say, "I'll have to go ask."

Bank tellers have to go ask somebody if they can cash a second-party check. Cash-register operators have to call a supervisor to okay a check. The accountant has to get permission to remove a $1.99 interest charge from a bill.

Why?

We've all seen a check-out clerk keep a line of six customers waiting while the manager gets off the phone, saunters over, glances at the check the customer wrote, circles the driver's license number and phone number, and initials it, all the while talking about where he is going for lunch.

What did that manager do that the check-out clerk couldn't?

What does requiring the clerk to call the manager over say to the employee about his judgment skills?

We're talking self-esteem.

Some organizations compound the problem by using their front-line employees as a screening device.

Have you ever tried to return an item, and had the sales clerk say, "We don't give cash refunds to people who don't have receipts. People come in here all the time with items purchased two years ago and want a refund. My manager said we can give a credit, but no cash refund."

If you complain, you're told, "I'll call my manager."

Eventually, the manager appears and asks, "What's the problem?"

You repeat your request for a cash refund.

"Okay, give it to her," the manager says when you are done going through your story for a second time.

With resentment toward this front-line clerk, you walk away with your refund. Companies that have policies like this always make the front-line people feel like the bad guys.

If, on occasion, you're going to make exceptions to your policies, let lower-level employees make those exceptions. Give them the judgment skills or training required and let them be more than a smoke screen.

That's why our drivers don't say to a customer who has a problem with an order, "You'll have to call customer service about that." Instead the driver picks up the phone in the presence of the customer and says, *"I've* got a customer here with a problem and *I'd* like to help them."

It does wonders for an employee's self-esteem to be the one to make a customer happy. You don't increase anyone's self-esteem by making them say, "I'll have to ask."

If you are worried about employees giving away the store, you can put spending limits on their authority. Beyond one hundred dollars, for example, they *will* have to check with someone, but up until their spending limit, it's their call. What we are talking about is giving employees more than a tiptoe hold on their job. We're talking about *empowerment,* the most obvious sign of respect for the employee.

You can empower people in innumerable ways. You can teach them better social skills. You can introduce them to others so they develop "connections." You can use your influence to persuade others to grant them more power because of their connection to you. You can enlarge their responsibilities. And you can empower them by letting them be the good guys.

Here's how we empower our employees.

They can issue a credit without having the returned merchandise in hand.

Our customer-service reps can decide whether to drop the freight charges, to hire a courier for special delivery, or to get in their car and deliver the package themselves.

Our managers can hire and terminate without approval or screening from the higher-ups.

Our supervisors can decide on the spot to pay a customer for damages—even if we didn't do the damage.

Here's what I mean. A customer calls and says, "Your truck backed over my esplanade of plants. I'm going to bill you for the damages." Now even if our supervisor goes out to the site and verifies by the tire tracks that our driver didn't do the damage, the supervisor can okay the payment. The reasoning? What's four hundred dollars in light of keeping a customer?

If you have a slogan that says, "Do whatever it takes to satisfy a customer," or, "The customer is always right," or, "Your satisfaction guaranteed or your money back," you haven't exactly spelled out the rules. You're creating an awful lot of confusion if you don't intend to let employees decide what it takes to "satisfy" the customer. It is a whole lot easier to let the players out in the field make the call.

Respect for the individual means letting them think and act. You've misnamed the department if customer-service reps "have to go ask someone" before they can satisfy the customer.

## REQUIRE ACCOUNTABILITY: THE OTHER SIDE OF THE COIN

Along with empowerment comes accountability. We've kept enough records throughout the years to know approximately how long it will take to install a furniture order. The foreman works with us to determine the labor cost for an installation, and he calls the plays on how to get the job done. If his people stand around for an hour before they get to the job site, we can't bill the client for that time. We eat it, and the foreman has to explain to us what happened. He has control, and we respect his judgment. But along with that authority comes responsibility. That's accountability.

On large orders our sales reps receive their commission when we get paid. So if they foul up the paperwork, or create other problems that cause the customers to be late in paying, their commission is delayed as well. If they make a mistake in ordering furniture, and the customer refuses to accept it, we give the salesperson 120 days to resell it. If they can't, we require them to pay for half the order. That's accountability, too.

Accountability goes hand in hand with empowerment. We want to empower our people to think and act. If they act in ways that make the customer happy, they are rewarded; all our revenue-generating departments are on commission.

What do workers really want from their employers? I don't think it is all that hard to figure out. Over the years, our people have told me that they want:

- to be treated fairly
- to be trusted
- to be judged by the work they do
- to have their say
- to have a chance to grow
- to work for a growing company

Contrary to my former boss's light-switch analogy, employees are not overhead. They are appreciating assets to be maintained, loved, and empowered.

## COACH'S CHECKLIST

✔ *Believe in the worth of your employees.* Show that you sincerely believe in them by speaking to them, smiling at them, and asking about their lives.

✔ *Empower your employees.* Don't put them in the position of having to say, "I'll have to go ask." Show that you respect their judgment. Give them the authority to make decisions. But along with that authority, give them accountability as well. When they have accountability *and* authority, they are truly empowered.

✔ *Keep your promises.* If you don't, you will have lost their respect as well as your credibility.

# Huddle on the First Day

> *A company is known by the people it keeps.*

"OH . . . YOU. You're here. Great. Right on time. Come on, I'll take you down to your work area."

Boss and new hire trudge along the hallway together.

"Well, this is it. Let me introduce you to a few people." The boss starts guiding the new hire around the department. The new employee is introduced to a number of people—so many, in fact, that there is no way to remember who anyone is. And then the tour is complete, and the boss guides the new hire to an empty desk.

"I put a copy of the employee handbook in your desk drawer. Look through it, and if you have any questions, ask someone to interpret it for you."

"Thanks, I will."

"Okay."

"Well, I'll leave you alone to get settled in. Call me if you need anything or have any questions."

Sound familiar?

It should, as that is the typical first-day experience for a new employee in most corporations. Off to the wrong start. Or should I say, off to no start.

Studies show hiring a new employee costs an average of six thousand dollars. And 60 percent of those new hires leave their jobs within the first seven months! How new employees are treated on their first day has to be a contributing factor. That *first day* makes an indelible impression that affects long-term performance. Quite frankly, it is the *most important day* in an employee's career. It sets the tone for everything that will follow. How employees are treated on their first day is something every manager should make a top priority.

If you've just spent six thousand dollars to woo someone, you've got to win them quickly. Shaking a few hands will not make them feel wanted. Asking them to glance through the employee handbook when they have time and ask someone if they have questions won't make them feel special.

Happy, satisfied employees work harder. What new hire is really going to ask the boss, "Who's got the real power around here?" or "I've got to have two days off in late fall for minor surgery—what's the sick policy?" No one is going to ask those things within hours of showing up at a new job. Still, these are exactly the kinds of things that people want to know. You have to find ways to convey that information.

With six thousand dollars on the line, consider an employee's early days at your company a probation period—for both you and the new hire. Do everything you can to make coming to work for you memorable and comfortable. Make new employees feel that they are part of your family—your team—from the very first day they arrive.

## GIVE THEM A FAMILY WELCOME

The first thing we do is send a "welcome to the team" letter to the *home* of new employees *before* their first day. Why to their home? We want their family and friends to see how important that new employee is. The letter welcomes them to our family and our team and tells them they are special.

And long before those employees arrive for their first day at work, we will have planned a complete agenda for their first few weeks. The employee's supervisor will create a detailed orientation and/or training schedule, based on the new employee's history.

We don't expect new people to have to "nose around" to find out how we do business. We want our players on the field as soon as possible, so they can learn first-hand what their job is all about.

We schedule two orientation sessions for new employees. The first is held during the first day of work, when a member of our human-resources department sits down with them, and on a one-to-one basis, goes over every single page of the employee handbook. We want people to know everything they possibly can about our policies and benefits, and we won't let new employees leave that one-to-one meeting until we have answered *all* their questions.

Our second orientation session occurs later. I spend about two hours with the new employees reviewing the background and philosophies of the company. The purpose of this orientation is to motivate and inspire.

As chairman of the board, I could try to overwhelm them with facts and figures—such as how we've grown from $50,000 to $150 million in sales in twenty-five years and from three employees to more than six hundred. But what good would it do? They already know we are a successful company, otherwise they wouldn't have applied for the job. They also know, thanks to the rigorous screening process we put them through before we hired them, that we attribute our success to the quality of people we hire.

Instead of repeating things they already know, I stress what it takes to be successful at our company. The first thing that new employees are given during this two-hour orientation is a Success Kit. In it they find:

*A bottle of enthusiasm.* This bottle, filled with a green (nonalcoholic) liquid is labeled: "Highly effective for success. For relief of apathy due to lack of interest and excitement. Dosage: As needed daily or hourly. Warnings: Can cause a new outlook on life; success." I always tell the group, "It will make you feel terrific as soon as you take a swig." To illustrate, I chug-a-lug the whole bottle in front of them. "Whenever you've had a difficult day, the prescription on the front of the bottle instructs you to take a little, or a lot. *Refills are free.*" In reality, the "magic" green liquid is water with green food coloring. Its "magic" is strictly the positive thinking that it inspires.

*A pen imprinted with "TERRIFIC!"* This pen goes a long way toward communicating our expectations of a positive attitude.

If you ask a dozen people during the day "How are you?" over 75 percent will answer "Fine." When someone says *"Terrific,"* faces break into smiles. First, their enthusiasm—either aided by the green liquid or not—is contagious. Second, people want to know what you've been up to when you respond with an enthusiastic *"Terrific."* We want our vendors and our customers to catch our positive attitude. *"Terrific"* has become the password around our building. If you ask anyone at our companies how they are doing, they'll usually answer: *"Terrific!"* Not "Fine."

*A piece of string.* The string is my way of helping new employees understand a key point about our company.

Here's how it works. They receive a twelve-inch piece of string and I say, "I'll give the first person who can push the string from one side of the desk to the other in a straight line a hundred-dollar bill." Everyone's motivated, of course, but no one can do it. You can't push a piece of string. It coils and resists.

It's the same with people. If you push people, they resist. You can lead *willing* people along with you, by coaching, training, answering questions, and helping them. But you can't push them, and indeed we won't. Somebody who has to be pushed has the wrong attitude.

*A mirror.* The mirror, framed in cardboard, says, "I believe in myself. The best is yet to come." This mirror is my way of saying that their success on the job depends on them.

At this point in my presentation I always tell about some of our employees who joined our team in an entry-level position and moved to the top. For example, our manager of data-processing started out as a driver. Our vice president of operations at Business Interiors began as a shipping clerk. More than eighty employees have been promoted to positions better than their entry-level position when they started their career with us. The point? The new hires know that their attitude and commitment can take them wherever they want to go in our company.

The mirror also serves as a lead-in to a poem that is very important to me. It's called "The Man in the Glass," and its author is unknown. The poem summarizes my philosophy of life, and I hope it also will become our employees' credo. We all have a common denominator: *each day we all have to look in the mirror.*

### THE MAN IN THE GLASS

*When you get what you want in your struggle for self*
*And the world makes you king for a day,*
*Just go to a mirror and look at yourself*
*And see what that man has to say.*

*For it isn't your father, mother, or wife*
*Whose judgment upon you must pass*
*The fellow whose verdict counts most in your life,*
*Is the one staring back from the glass.*

*Some people may think you a straight-shootin' chum*
*And call you a wonderful guy,*
*But the man in the glass says you're only a bum—*
*If you can't look him straight in the eye.*

*He's the fellow to please—never mind all the rest,*
*For he's with you clear up to the end.*
*And you've passed your most dangerous, difficult test*
*If the man in the glass is your friend.*

*You may fool the whole world down the pathway of life*
*And get pats on your back as you pass,*
*But your final reward will be heartaches and tears—*
*If you've cheated the man in the glass.*

*—Anonymous*

Toward the end of my talk, I give everyone a personalized *Million Dollar Certificate* that guarantees they'll feel like a million if they follow daily the ten principles printed on it. I review all ten points with them. The certificate can be found on the page 187.

Immediately after my talk, a letter from me goes to the employee's home thanking him or her for attending, and reconfirming my desire to have an ongoing line of communication between management and employees. (You'll note this is the second letter, in a short time, that the employee has received at home.)

By now we've communicated to new employees that their arrival was worth preparing for—it was a big deal. But we don't stop there. We also assign them to a "buddy" for thirty days.

That buddy can be from any area of the company, but it will be someone on the employee's level. We don't pair warehouse people

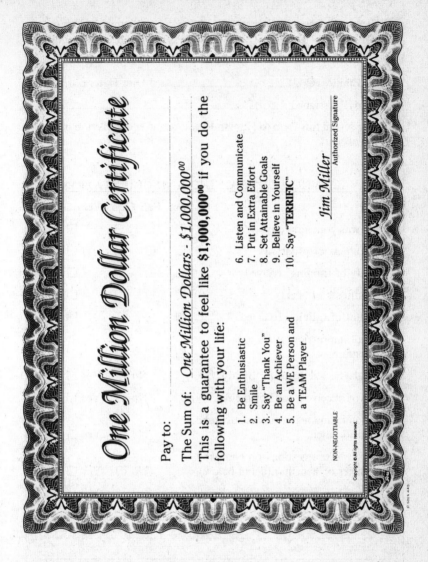

*One Million Dollar Certificate*

Pay to: _____

The Sum of:  *One Million Dollars - $1,000,000⁰⁰*

This is a guarantee to feel like **$1,000,000⁰⁰** if you do the following with your life:

1. Be Enthusiastic
2. Smile
3. Say "Thank You"
4. Be an Achiever
5. Be a WE Person and a TEAM Player

6. Listen and Communicate
7. Put in Extra Effort
8. Set Attainable Goals
9. Believe in Yourself
10. Say "TERRIFIC"

*Jim Miller*
Authorized Signature

NON-NEGOTIABLE

Copyright © All rights reserved.

with executive vice presidents. The buddy answers any questions, usually the behind-the-scenes stuff not addressed in the employee manual. New employees will feel a lot more comfortable asking a buddy what constitutes sick leave than they would be asking their immediate boss.

On that first day of work, the buddy and the employee's boss take

## *How Was Your First Week?*

New Employee: _____    Hire Date: _____

"Buddy" Assigned: _____

Please return this form to Human Resources after completion of one week of work.

### EVALUATION OF TRAINING AND ORIENTATION

|  | Poor | Fair | Good | Very Good |
|---|---|---|---|---|
| How was your first day? | ☐ | ☐ | ☐ | ☐ |
| Helpfulness of program | ☐ | ☐ | ☐ | ☐ |
| Quality of training received | ☐ | ☐ | ☐ | ☐ |
| Friendliness of peers | ☐ | ☐ | ☐ | ☐ |
| Amount of training received | ☐ | ☐ | ☐ | ☐ |
| Overall impression of training program | ☐ | ☐ | ☐ | ☐ |

| | |
|---|---|
| Would you like to be a "Buddy"? | No ☐    Yes ☐ |
| Did you receive a tour of the facility? | No ☐    Yes ☐ |
| Did your manager/supervisor take you to lunch? | No ☐    Yes ☐ |
| Do you have questions on company policies or benefits? (detail below) | No ☐    Yes ☐ |

Comments: _____

_____

_____

_____

_____

_____    _____
Signature—New Employee                   Date

the new employee to lunch at the company's expense. The buddy or the manager also gives the new employee a tour of the facilities and makes introductions to *all* our employees—their teammates—along the way.

From the very beginning, we want to create a family atmosphere.

We put a lot of time and effort into planning our employees' first days with us, and we want to know if the new employees feel they got anything out of it. At the end of the first week, we have the new person complete an evaluation form entitled, *How Was Your First Week?* A copy of this form appears on page 188.

Having them fill out the form does two things. First, it shows that we care how they feel. Second, it says that this company wants them to talk back and let us know what is going on.

After the first thirty days, new employees give us feedback again, this time on whether or not their buddy met their needs.

## CALL A NEW HUDDLE ON PROMOTION DAY

It's always a good idea to repeat the orientation process when employees are promoted. Review their responsibilities in their new role and reemphasize the team-coach philosophy. Say something like: "Here's your new title, your paycheck, and your new piece of string. You will get more out of your team if you lead them instead of pushing them."

This is the procedure we always follow. However, on occasion the symbolism doesn't work.

A few years ago, as I walked through the warehouse one morning, I heard a new supervisor screaming at the top of his lungs, "You idiot, don't do it that way!" Five minutes later, I heard him yelling at someone else, so I called him into my office.

I asked him, "What was the problem?" He mumbled something about how his co-workers didn't respond to his orders.

"I'm going to do you a favor. Since you are having a little trouble out there with your people, I want to see if I can give you some help."

"Good. I could use some."

I reached in my desk drawer and pulled out a sign. "I'm going to place this sign around your neck, and I want you to wear it for the rest of the day."

The sign said, I'M THE BOSS. I walked over and put it around his neck. The sign came to rest on his chest.

"You wouldn't do that!"

"I already have. Your employees evidently don't understand your role yet. Now they'll know you're boss. You won't have to yell at them, as the sign tells them that you are the boss."

I didn't know if my idea would work. Odds were he would get angry and quit. But I was hoping he'd learn something about management and stay.

He fumed for a minute or two, and then I said, "I also have another sign, one I hope you'll prefer to wear in the future."

The second sign was one that said COACH.

I told him he would get more out of his employees if he acted as their coach. He needed to advise, direct, and encourage his team, not shout at them.

He got the point . . . and stayed.

Those first-day huddles, whether that first day is when a new employee joins your company or when they begin a new job, serve to show people what you expect from them and what they can expect from you in the way of support.

The huddle also emphasizes their role on the team. When they see their boss treating them with integrity, sincerity, and empathy, they know that's how their boss wants them to act as well. We want them to share our company values, feel ownership, and "talk up" the organization to their family and friends.

From day one, you have to communicate that you care about the people who work with you. A caring atmosphere builds loyalty.

## COACH'S CHECKLIST

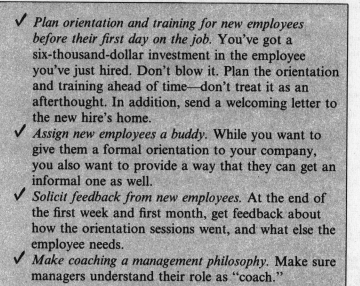

✓ *Plan orientation and training for new employees before their first day on the job.* You've got a six-thousand-dollar investment in the employee you've just hired. Don't blow it. Plan the orientation and training ahead of time—don't treat it as an afterthought. In addition, send a welcoming letter to the new hire's home.

✓ *Assign new employees a buddy.* While you want to give them a formal orientation to your company, you also want to provide a way that they can get an informal one as well.

✓ *Solicit feedback from new employees.* At the end of the first week and first month, get feedback about how the orientation sessions went, and what else the employee needs.

✓ *Make coaching a management philosophy.* Make sure managers understand their role as "coach."

# 2 4

# Create What They Miss at Home

> *"People who need people are the luckiest people in the world."*

FAMILY MEANS emotional support, love, and encouragement to be our best. Or should I say, that's what families traditionally have meant. But since our families are no longer traditional—thanks to the rapid rise in the number of divorces, single-parent families, commuter marriages, and the like—the person at the next desk has become family for many people. And even in traditional homes, employees often spend more waking hours with each other than they do with their families.

Because this is the case today, the time you spend with the people you work with should be enjoyable. Take time to get together every once in a while just to have fun. We do.

Once a month, our departments have a potluck lunch. Often, it's not the eating together but the planning that is most fun. Whether it's a picnic, barbecue, or contest celebration, they work together as a team to plan every detail.

Sometimes our employees set up their own social get-togethers after hours. Recently, a number of our employees and their spouses took their vacations together and went skiing in Colorado.

## GET PERSONAL

Families traditionally offer support in all areas of your life. We try to do that too. When our sales managers conduct performance reviews, they check on the progress the employees are making on their personal as well as professional goals: "Have you built that deck yet?" "Did you start that second savings account?" "What's your golf handicap these days?" These are personal subjects employees have shared with their managers and want encouragement on.

Some people don't want to mix their personal and business lives. Some, but not many. Obviously, if people are uncomfortable talking about their life outside of work, we don't pry. But we've found most people are happy—and want—to talk about what they are doing beyond their job.

If your employees do want to "open up," make the environment in which you hold your conversations as comfortable as possible. Our marketing director at Business Interiors takes her employees off-site for performance reviews. At a breakfast or lunch, employees feel more comfortable in sharing difficulties they're having or in asking for help on the job. Because criticism has a longer life than praise, we focus on what employees are doing right in these sessions.

The flip side involves encouraging employees to care about their colleagues and communities. While some organizations view personal involvement in civic functions and charitable fund-raisers as "time away from the job," we encourage it. Besides giving something back to the community that helped us become successful, we're underscoring for our people the need to help people less fortunate than themselves.

Writing a check won't cut it. People need to participate personally—whether competing to see how much money their team can raise during a walkathon or collecting toys for a women's shelter.

This charitable attitude spills over to each other on the job too. Our furniture company had a sales contest called the World-Class Championship Challenge in which salespeople received fake two-dollar bills for their sales volume as rewards. They also received a pack of fake bills as giveaways for other employees, who went out of their way to help them in their sales efforts. At the end of the four-month contest, the idea was for everyone to write their names on the back of the two-dollar bills they had received and toss them into drawings for prizes at the company-wide picnic.

But you know what happened? Most of the people "endorsed" their two-dollar bills over to fellow employees and tossed those names into the drawings, rather than their own name! A warehouse employee won a color television. A $250 gift certificate for exercise equipment went to one of the secretaries. This was their "best selves" in action. That's the kind of spirit teamwork fosters.

Families also provide emotional support. *People need people.* Over time, that statement has been reduced to a cliché, but that doesn't detract from its truth. People have to feel that whatever the problem, others will care enough to help.

Some problems are easy to solve.

My wife got a call one day from a distraught employee, "I've just run over a cat—what do I do?"

Another employee was depressed because her daughter needed dental work and she couldn't find an orthodontist who would take her on as a patient unless she paid for half of the work up front. With a few phone calls, we found an orthodontist for her who would work with her on a time-payment schedule that she could handle.

A monumental problem becomes a bit smaller, if you just have someone to ask. And that someone can be a fellow employee, as well as a manager.

Our employees have helped one another move into new homes, care for sick kids, give emotional support through divorces, and plan weddings. Last Christmas, one employee's car was broken into at work and all his kids' Christmas presents were stolen out of it. Our employees raised eighteen hundred dollars to replace the toys.

When one of our top account executives was seriously ill for more than two years, five of our reps pitched in to take care of his accounts while he was ill.

We've even had a sales rep, who had never had children, serve as a Lamaze coach for her fellow sales rep, during a husband's out-of-town trip. One of our workers, whose wife is a nurse, helped a colleague deliver her child when they got stuck in traffic on their way to the hospital. Mother, child, and co-worker came through it all fine.

Through the years, we've prayed for our employees—a mother whose baby had a serious heart defect; longtime employees suffering from cancer; parents with sons and daughters off at war; a colleague whose spouse was tragically killed. In the most vivid incident, the entire company prayed for two days for a Business Interiors employee who was kidnapped and held hostage by an armed intruder who had broken into her home. (She eventually escaped unharmed.)

What matters is that they feel emotional support from those they work with every day.

You can have all kinds of formal counseling programs available—and we do. But in addition to professional help, employees need to see that the people around them are concerned—whether through prayers, money during a crisis, or giving of their personal time. Employees have to be there for each other off the playing field. Concern can't be wrapped up in an eight-hour day.

If an employee calls me after hours to say, "I'm having problems with my sixteen-year-old; can I come by and talk to you about it?" You bet they can. We want all our employees to answer the same way.

One of my favorite poems, "That Man Is a Success," expresses this very well. People have to succeed as human beings before they can succeed as employees or anything else.

## THAT MAN IS A SUCCESS

*Who has lived well,
  laughed often and loved much;*

*Who has gained the respect
  of intelligent men and the love of children;*

*Who has filled his niche
  and accomplished his task;*

*Who leaves the world better than he found it,
  whether by an improved poppy, a perfect poem or a rescued
  soul;*

*Who never lacked appreciation
  of earth's beauty or failed to express it;*

*Who looked for the best in others
  and gave the best he had.*

—*Bessie Anderson Stanley*

Also, like members of a family, employees need strong leaders. Leaders who have vision. Leaders who encourage and inspire. Leaders who can serve as role models. Leaders who build pride in others about their achievements.

Of course, as in families, there can be jealousies and personality conflicts, disagreements and squabbles. And those are handled in the usual ways. Open communication works wonders even with jealousies and disagreements.

## HUGS HELP

> *"Remember, you've got a boss who loves you."*

But most important of all, a work family gives a sense of belonging. Frequently, I'll tell employees, "Remember, you've got a boss who loves you."

Yes, love. Not a comment expressed often in the workplace, but one that employees need to hear. The "hugging professor," Leo Buscaglia, writes about it. So does Jess Lair in *I Ain't Much, Baby, But I'm All I Got,* a book that brought home to me the point about caring for people you work with. The late Vince Lombardi also instilled in his players the importance of caring. "We're a successful team," Lombardi used to say, "because we love each other."

Love—a profoundly motivating emotion.

I always talk about this in speeches I give around the country. After one speech, an audience member sent me a newspaper story with the headline "College Embraces Hug Therapy to Blunt Soaring Suicide Trends." The article was about how Sinclair Community College, in Dayton, Ohio, was advocating the idea that hugs prevent suicide.

Hugs do help. If employees don't have loving support at home, they desperately need it at work. What the world needs is a good hug.

Does the family atmosphere work? 3M thinks so. Hewlett Packard thinks so. Disney thinks so. Many exemplary companies think so. In many instances the family atmosphere at work helps offset the lack of a traditional family atmosphere at home.

The value of a work family is often reflected day to day in employees' attitudes about the company.

Several years ago, we had torrential rain that caved in one of our warehouse roofs at 2:00 A.M. Our service manager was there all night trying to protect as much inventory as possible from the storm. When one of the hourly employees learned about the disaster, he phoned the people he worked with in the warehouse, and they showed up within minutes to help move the inventory. Hourly employees coming in to work in the middle of the night just to help! They cared.

Our absenteeism rate is one-third less than the national average. Our turnover rate is 5 percent annually. At other service companies nationwide it's about five times that.

Turnover and absenteeism cost money; being concerned about each other costs nothing.

And, as I've said, 35 percent of our employees come from employee referrals, from people who say "Miller's or Business Interiors is a good place to work; it has a family atmosphere." We encourage our employees to have their relatives apply here. They talk about us at the dinner table, adding another level of emotional support for each other.

The less people sense they're cared for by those around them, the more time and energy they'll focus on "looking out for number one." That's something that neither you—nor they—need.

Invest in the personal lives of your people. Make them feel like family, and they'll act like family.

## COACH'S CHECKLIST

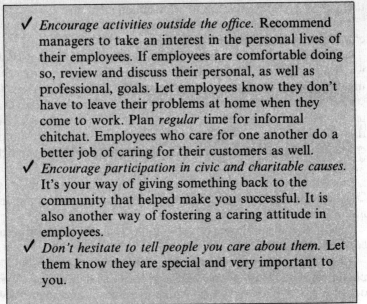

✓ *Encourage activities outside the office.* Recommend managers to take an interest in the personal lives of their employees. If employees are comfortable doing so, review and discuss their personal, as well as professional, goals. Let employees know they don't have to leave their problems at home when they come to work. Plan *regular* time for informal chitchat. Employees who care for one another do a better job of caring for their customers as well.

✓ *Encourage participation in civic and charitable causes.* It's your way of giving something back to the community that helped make you successful. It is also another way of fostering a caring attitude in employees.

✓ *Don't hesitate to tell people you care about them.* Let them know they are special and very important to you.

# 25

# Make Them Heroes in Front of Family and Friends

> *The greatest good we can do for others is not to share our own riches, but to reveal theirs.*

ONE THING about the family atmosphere that we *don't* want to duplicate is the tendency to take family members for granted. Family members don't always recognize and praise each other's accomplishments. My father's favorite line used to be, "If you mess up, I'll tell you." But I longed to hear him tell me when I did things just right.

That's our goal at work. We want to tell people when they do something right. Recognition goes a long way toward creating satisfied employees, and satisfied employees will perform well for customers.

Look for heroes in every area of your company, and make them models for underachievers.

Here's what we do. We select and reward the Administrative Employee of the Month, Customer-Service Team of the Month, Sales Employee of the Month, Sales Support Employee of the Month, Design Employee of the Month, Purchasing/Rental Customer-Service Employee of the Month, Accounting Employee of the Month, Delivery Employee of the Month, Installer of the Month, and others.

You're limited only by the number of award titles you can think of.

At Business Interiors, as part of our recognition and rewards, the winners get to play our own version of *Let's Make a Deal*. Employees can choose to take what they win—for being employee of the month, for example—or gamble that they can win something better in the drawing that is held each quarter for people who have won a monthly award.

Be creative in your criteria for winning. Granted, it's much easier to identify appropriate criteria for salespeople than for truck drivers. But it's possible. Besides, the criteria you come up with may spur your thinking about ways to increase line output or improve attendance.

Here are some of the things we do. We give awards for new accounts opened. We may give a bonus for "lines pulled" in the warehouse, or for most outstanding receivables collected. Drivers can earn up to a thousand-dollar bonus for accident-free periods.

You get the picture. Try to make heroes of people for their successes.

# 26

# Create Small Wins

> *"You've been caught doing something good!"*

ON OCCASION, you'll want to reward people immediately—no waiting until the end of the month or the end of the quarter. You'll want to tell people *today* that they did a *terrific* job.

A group of installers worked thirty-six hours straight to get a job done on time, so we gave each of them two tickets to a Texas Rangers game. On a particularly intricate job in the Bahamas that was going to keep our installers away from home for a while, we paid for their spouses to fly down to join them on a cruise once the work was done.

Another immediate award—we call them small wins—that employees appreciate is receiving the *You've Been Caught Doing Something Good!* or *You Are Terrific* certificates that they can display in their workstation, on their computer terminal, or in their truck. When someone—anyone in our company—catches someone else doing something exceptional, they can issue one of these certificates, which you will find on pages 202 and 204.

Employees send them for any number of reasons. Our vice president of marketing sent one to a data-processing employee for setting up a specialized reporting form on her own time. A sales rep sent one to a warehouse staffer for contacting vendors and getting special samples of products he needed. The director of human resources gave one to a member of her staff for creatively rigging a

**BUSINESS INTERIORS®**
*"We strive to be your office solutions company."*

# YOU'VE BEEN CAUGHT . . .
# DOING SOMETHING GOOD!

To:

Thanks For:

From _____    Signature _____    Date _____
    (Please Print)

Their Supervisor _____

White: Recipient    Canary: Their Supervisor    Pink: John Sample                    27YBHB-08/91 computer program that allowed us to get our payroll out on time. The tele-serve manager received one for handling 834 calls during a three-week sales blitz. The president and executive vice president of Business Interiors received one for giving the accounting department a day off for exceptional work.

Our furniture company has created a novel approach to vary the instant recognition of employees who are "caught" providing a level of service above and beyond simply qualifying for a certificate. A tiny gray felt "Koality Bear" clutching a crisp five-dollar bill in its paws is given to the employee, who may collect a number of the bears and turn them in for prizes at a later date.

Big wins, small wins. From the bottom. From the top. From the boss. From the mail clerk. Givers of the awards are the sole judge of who deserves them.

At best, the certificates may influence a pay raise or promotion. At the least, they bring a satisfied smile, and make someone's week.

There's one other thing to note about these awards. Copies are sent to management. If you receive a *You Are Terrific* certificate, a copy goes to the human-resources department, which places it in your permanent file, and a copy goes to Mike Miller, the company president. At Business Interiors, not only does a copy of the *You've Been Caught Doing Something Good!* go to your supervisor, one also goes to company president, John Sample.

## ATTACH VALUE AT THE TOP

Any company who doesn't have formal recognition systems in place will have some questions: First, do they work? Second, how do you make small awards, like certificates, meaningful? Third, does the value of the awards decrease because you are giving them out so frequently?

The answers to all three questions depends on the attitude of the people at the top of the organization. If the awards are important to senior management, they're important to everyone else.

I don't care how high up the corporate ladder people climb, they appreciate recognition of their expertise and successes. Internationally, we honor Nobel Prize and Pulitzer Prize winners. We award foundation money to outstanding researchers. We grant sabbati-

MILLER
BUSINESS
SYSTEMS, INC.

## Quest For Excellence

# YOU ARE TERRIFIC!

**Special Recognition is hereby given to:**

_____          _____
Name                             Department                        Title

**Reason for Recognition:**

☐ Excellent Customer Service      ☐ Excellent Suggestion            ☐ Perfect Attendance
☐ Excellence in Work Performance  ☐ Terrific Job Attitude           ☐ Zero Defects
☐ Saving Money                    ☐ Outstanding Personal Conduct    ☐ Saving Time

**Describe briefly what events or special efforts were involved:** _____

_____

_____

_____

_____
Manager/Supervisor Signature

cc: Human Resources

MILLER
BUSINESS
SYSTEMS, INC.
QUEST
FOR
EXCELLENCE

cals to honored professors. In our professional organizations, we elect the "Person of the Year," "Manager of the Year," "Outstanding Engineer of the Year," "Trainer of the Year," "Mentor of the Year." You name it and we honor it.

If you want your awards to be taken seriously, include top management among the recipients. Two years ago, we established the Presidential Award, called the "M-ie," which went to the two vice presidents who organized, launched, and now direct our quality program.

The awards around here—whether they are a reserved parking space in the front of the building, free aerobic classes, photos in the local paper, or receiving a *You Are Terrific* or *You've Been Caught Doing Something Good!* certificate—are appreciated by all.

## MAKE A BIG SPLASH WITH THE ANNOUNCEMENT

If you are going to recognize someone for doing a good job, make a big deal about it. Announce it over the public-address system. Put up posters or a banner.

Sometimes recognition can be conveyed simply by personal attention from senior management. Examples? The vice president of operations asks three people from the warehouse to have lunch with him to say thank you for all the outstanding ideas they submitted through the quality program. The president arranges a catered lunch and eats with the order pullers to thank them for their great attitude during a peak work load.

Don't underestimate the value of personal time and attention as rewards.

And when your team generates an exciting idea, why not have them all make the formal presentation to management? Again, that's personal recognition for their individual contributions.

## SEND 'EM HOME IN GLORY

When our senior executives and managers write letters to our employees for doing something exceptional, those letters are sent to the employees' homes. Or we send flowers—to the homes of both men and women—to say thanks for a job well done on a special project.

Why to their homes? Some employees don't feel comfortable tooting their own horn at home, so we help them become heroes to their families. That bouquet of flowers sitting on the kitchen table will prompt a seven-year-old to ask, "What did you do to get this, Dad?"

Or that letter of commendation in the mailbox will get a spouse to say, "I didn't know that project you've been working on was so important—this is from the president, isn't it?"

Simple gestures, yes; common gestures, no. In my own informal surveys of audiences over the years, I've found that *less than 2 percent* of employees have ever received a letter at their home from senior management complimenting them for a job well done.

It costs only pennies to send a letter or a card to employees' homes. They will show this letter to their family, relatives, and friends, but most important, they will feel they are appreciated.

## MAKE BIRTHDAYS A SPECIAL EVENT

A friend of mine in New Jersey phoned me one day and asked, "Do you have stock in Hallmark?"

"No. Should I?"

I thought he was about to give me a stock tip. He didn't. He went on to tell me how much money he had spent in the last twelve months sending birthday cards to his employees' homes. It was an idea that he borrowed from us, as every one of our employees gets a personal birthday card signed by the president.

"Just last week a fellow stopped me in the hall and thanked me for sending the card," my friend told me. "Said he'd worked for the company for thirty-five years and that this was the first time anybody at the company had ever wished him a happy birthday."

"This is one of the best investments I've ever made in my employees," my friend told me.

It was a simple, inexpensive gesture, and one that the employee will remember forever.

If I am in town, I will lead the employees in singing "Happy Birthday."

What can you do to make your employees' work meaningful to them? If you can't make it meaningful, can you make it fun? If you can't make it fun, can you make it high-profile? If you can't make it high-profile, can you make it profitable? What healthy competition can you devise to stimulate recognition, fun, profits, and performance? What can you do that will underscore for your employees how important their jobs actually are? What can you do to turn them into heroes in the eyes of their family and friends?

Happy employees do a better job. There's a great story that captures this concept. Three workers at a construction site are asked how they spend their days.

The first said, "I'm making a living." The second replied, "I'm cutting stone." The third answered, "I'm building a cathedral."

Recognition turns work projects into cathedrals.

Heroes feel like winners, perform like winners, and serve customers like winners.

## COACH'S CHECKLIST

> ✓ *Encourage employees to believe in themselves.* Do everything in your power to publicize their successes.
> ✓ *Let everyone recognize good work.* Every single employee at your company should be able to praise—in some kind of formal way—all of the other people he or she works with.
> ✓ *Have the boss give the award, whenever possible.* Praise from a peer is good; recognition from top management is better.
> ✓ *Praise them at home, too.* Make employees heroes at home by sending letters, flowers, tickets to a ball game, or other presents to the house.

# 27

# Remember: Teams That Play Together Stay Together

> *If you enjoy your job, you never have to go to work.*

ONE OF the things I firmly believe is: "If you enjoy your job, you'll never have to go to work." Too many people wake up every morning wishing they were doing some other type of job. They aren't happy. That's why we try to make going to work as much fun as we can. We want *all* our employees to enjoy their jobs. Happy employees are productive employees.

Let me tell you about a few of the things we do:

*Spirit days:* The second Friday of every month, our customer service department comes to work in their team T shirt and jeans. The entire office dresses in casual attire on that day.

If clothes make the man, clothes can *unmake* him—or her. Clothes and attitude go together. Putting on a team T shirt and jeans puts people in the mood to relax and have fun. The people in Silicon Valley probably would add that casual dress enhances creativity and growth. Friends, fun, family, work—we want the images to blend.

I'm not suggesting making sweats or team T shirts a way of life. They're just for an occasional time-out. It's a change of pace that promotes productivity.

Now, we still have visitors come to our offices on Spirit Days. What do they think about seeing all our employees in T shirts and jeans? They love it. Just about every visitor says, "I wish we could do this at our company."

*Sandlot/parking lot games and company teams:* Sports contribute to the family feeling. On the ball field, players come to understand personalities that they'll have to deal with on the job the next day. They learn to pull together as a team. Playing sports helps develop a passion for winning. The physical workout is only a byproduct of the process. Is it any wonder that we sponsor company teams in almost every sport imaginable?

In addition, the guys in our warehouse take their morning and afternoon fifteen-minute breaks simultaneously. That gives them the opportunity to play touch football or basketball in the parking lot.

*Question:* "What do customers think when they drive by the parking lot and see a basketball game going on near the loading dock?"

*Answer:* "Wish I could take some of that fun back to where *I* work."

*Las Vegas night:* To show our appreciation for our employees, occasionally we've had a Las Vegas night, complete with shows, food, and gaming tables. People who win playing blackjack, roulette, or craps receive coupons that make them eligible for a drawing at the end of the evening for prizes like diamond rings and exotic trips.

*Potluck lunches and wine-and-cheese parties:* Every month, departments bring in potluck lunches to share, or arrange to have a caterer provide lunch. Occasionally they decide, for no reason other than "we deserve it," to change the potluck lunch to an after-work wine-and-cheese get-together off the premises.

*Appreciation breakfasts, lunches, and dinners for the support teams:* Whenever we finish a sales blitz, a big printing job, or a big installation, the people who were credited with doing the work like to thank their support staff, the behind-the-scenes people who made it all possible. So out of their own pockets, they plan get-togethers. A 6:00 A.M. breakfast in the warehouse for the delivery drivers, or a Mexican fiesta for the customer-service team.

Sometimes people even show their appreciation for the boss. Our Houston office decided they wanted to throw a party for their general manager, so they arranged a "This Is Your Life" presentation and invited all the executives from our Arlington office to come down for the day. Everyone had a terrific time.

*Halloween:* Halloween has become one of our biggest events of the year. Departments adopt a theme, decorate their part of the facilities, and dress "appropriately."

We've had people come to work as a roller-derby team, the Addams family, a box of colored crayons, and barnyard animals. (They covered the floor in their department with hay.) Everyone participates. Some of the costumes are so creative we can't tell who the employees are.

In addition to wearing costumes, we sponsor a pumpkin-carving contest where judges award cash prizes. All this encourages originality, creativity, and a sense of friendly competition among employees.

Our customers have been known to make a special trip to visit us on Halloween. (Even some of our customers and suppliers show up in costume.)

*Birthday celebrations:* Birthdays—anyone's birthday—mean food and balloons, crepe paper and streamers in the birthday person's department. (All this, of course, is in addition to the birthday cards we send them.)

When I was out of town for one of my birthdays, the employees decided to hold my party without me, and sent me a sixty-minute videotape where each department wished me a "Happy Birthday" in a very creative manner. Some tried their talents at songwriting, rapping, and acting, but they were all different. You can imagine the pleasure I received watching this film while I was on vacation. Six hundred employees wishing me Happy Birthday! That day at American Discount Office Furniture, my son Greg gave an extra 10 percent discount to anyone who called in and mentioned that they knew me, to help celebrate my birthday.

*Style shows:* Designers and architects share with employees and customers the latest in men's and women's fashions, fabrics, and furniture design. Food as exotic as the fashions—rattlesnake chili in tortilla cups, for example—is served, and everyone—customers and employees—has a great time.

*Opening night at Arlington Stadium:* On opening night of the Texas Rangers' baseball season, our employees and their families attend as a group. With over five hundred people attending last year, we made up more than 1 percent of the total attendance that night, and we created our own cheering sections.

*Six Flags' Christmas tree contests:* For an investment of between one thousand and fifteen hundred dollars—the money goes to charity—we sponsor a tree for our employees to decorate as part of a competition at the Six Flags over Texas amusement park. Employees spend hours together after work and on weekends planning and decorating this tree. Six Flags awards prizes for the "prettiest tree," "best theme," and more, and we often come home a winner.

*Corporate Challenge Championships:* More than 20 percent of our employees participate in the Corporate Challenge, sponsored by Hospital Corporation of America, in events that include swimming, softball, racquetball, golf, horseshoes, biking, jogging, basketball, darts, table tennis, bowling, tug-of-war, and volleyball tournaments throughout the year. In Arlington more than forty companies sponsor their firms in the Challenge. It's like being involved in the Olympics. The events are held over four weekends, and we compete against other firms to see which company wins the Corporate Challenge. Over the past years our team has done very well in the challenge. In addition to our participants, many other employees attend the competitive events to cheer for their teammates.

*Texas-style barbecues on the ranch:* On occasion, everybody exits the city and gathers in the country. We find a resort, a dude ranch, or somebody's uncle's farm, and have a cookout, complete with horseshoes and hay.

*Beef'n'beans contest:* Periodically, our sales teams put on a "beef'n'beans" contest. Two sales teams set a goal—the most furniture sold by a team in the next thirty days, or which team gets the most new office-supply accounts in a month, for example. The winning team dines on shrimp cocktail, steak with all the trimmings, and cherries jubilee. The losers get kidney-bean salad, a hot dog, baked beans, and jellybeans for dessert. The losing team sits across from the winners so that they can see close up that "to the winners go the spoils." The joy of winning . . . the agony of defeat.

*Safety tournaments:* You can even turn something as serious as safety into a fun event. Members of our safety team make unannounced visits to departments to question their colleagues: "Where's the closest fire extinguisher?" "Where's the nearest fire exit?" The most knowledgeable department wins a trophy. That is, until the team makes another inspection and the traveling trophy, an old fire extinguisher painted gold, moves to another department.

*Tour de Arlington:* As a fund-raiser for the Arlington Boys Club, we take part in a bicycle race around town. Typically, over one-fifth of our employees participate in the race, as well as help with the artwork and promotion. Again, more "together time."

*Contests of charitable fund-raisers:* We do all the usual things and then some: Walkathons, Toys for Tots, teddy bear collections for the local women's shelter, Boys Club, Girls Club, and more. People who learn to give to charities also give their commitment to customers.

Employees set their own pace on the fun. Teams generate the ideas, plan the details, and schedule the event. Every hour invested in a fun, positive atmosphere pays off in team productivity, employee loyalty, and better customer service down the road.

We don't care that our get-togethers often sound like pep rallies, complete with whoops, laughter, and applause. We want our employees to arrive and leave work feeling *terrific.*

Do you remember how many weeks in advance that you, as a third-grader, planned Valentine's Day card exchanges? Get in touch with the child inside you and have employees do the same. Corporate play heals employees' tired bodies and minds, and attracts customers the way a ball game attracts spectators.

*Let customers join the fun and games.* Our retail-store customers and visitors in our corporate offices can guess how many gadgets are in the jar on display—paper clips, erasers, staples, candy. The winners get a fifty-dollar gift certificate and their photo on our store bulletin board.

*Take the fun with you.* The year I was president of our trade association, we changed the format at our annual convention from structured social events to more casual fun, so that *all* the people attending could relax and enjoy the convention. Instead of our traditional president's reception, where people dressed to the nines to stand in line to greet the president and other officers, I convinced everyone we should have a "night at the ballpark," instead. We had the ballroom at the hotel set up as a baseball diamond, and hired an organist to play team songs. We ate peanuts, popcorn, and hot dogs. The people who normally stood in the receiving line wore the uniforms of their favorite baseball teams. The members didn't have to stand in any lines; they showed up at the reception and if they wanted to pay honor to an officer, they just went to the base where the officer stood. This eliminated the lines, and people were free to dress casually. It was a fun night.

Consider what you can turn into fun. On what holidays can you do something nontraditional to celebrate? What charitable activities can you make a party or contest?

Work should be fun. If it's not, it's just work.

### COACH'S CHECKLIST

✓ *Allow fun time for your employees.* Permit your employees some silly time to reduce stress and build camaraderie.

✓ *Organize fun with a purpose.* Use your celebrations to recognize employee achievement.

✓ *Share the fun.* Invite your customers to play with you.

# Always Ask Why When Players Leave to Become Free Agents

> *Turnover costs money. Concern costs nothing.*

**B**ACK IN 1967, shortly after we bought the business (as I explained in the first chapter), I took the three employees who "came with the store" to lunch to discuss how we, as a team, could turn things around. While we were waiting for our food, someone passed our table and spoke to one of our employees.

"Hi, Gary, how are you doing?"

Gary mumbled at him and made no eye contact.

The acquaintance added, "Nice to see you again. Where are you working now?"

Again Gary mumbled something unintelligible.

Not easily put off, the guy continued, "Sorry, what did you say?"

Gary mumbled for the third time. The guy finally got the hint and wandered off.

"Why did you do that?" I asked Gary, after the man had left.

"I didn't want him to know I still worked at Arlington Office Supply. We have the worst reputation in town."

"The worst reputation in town? There are only two office-supply stores in town!"

"No, I mean we've got the worst reputation of any business in any town."

That conversation confirmed my worst fears.

A company's reputation spills over onto its employees. They

either glow in the limelight or hide in the shadows. Getting them out in the limelight, where they can make customers happy, goes a long way toward making employees proud of where they work.

Today, as I've said, our employee turnover is 5 percent, while 20 percent is not uncommon in our industry. And what makes our average even more impressive is that it includes our warehouse, which operates three shifts a day. In a warehouse there tends to be a high annual turnover.

One of our most stable areas is our group of Business Interiors installers. The tenure for first-line supervisors there runs well over six years. I don't know of any other company in our industry that comes close to our record.

You should know how your turnover rate stacks up against other companies in your field. There should be thunder throughout the ranks if turnover begins to rise.

## DRAFT PLAYERS WITH THE EXPECTATION THEY'LL STAY ON THE TEAM

Our senior executives like to tell stories about the following: one of our vice presidents of operations who started out in the warehouse; a data-processing manager who began with us as a driver; a customer-service manager who started as a retail clerk; and a vice president and chief financial officer who started out as an accountant. The idea, of course, is to show employees that their potential for growth in our companies is virtually unlimited.

We recognize achievement with promotions, which gets employees to stick around for the finals. National statistics indicate employees will change jobs three to five times during a career, and many will have several careers. We hire people with the expectation that they'll stay forever.

We know recruiting, relocating, and training a replacement for each employee who leaves costs us about forty thousand dollars. Whatever that figure is in your own organization, keep it in the forefront of everyone's mind. Although that cost doesn't appear on your monthly profit-and-loss statement, employee turnover represents an expensive part of doing business.

## ASK THEM WHY WHEN THEY LEAVE

One of the best ways to get information that will help you create a work environment that will encourage people to stay is from the employees themselves. We pay a lot of attention to our annual employee surveys and exit interviews.

Exit interviews consist of a written questionnaire and a review of the completed questionnaire with someone from the human-resources department.

We find that the employees will be honest with you when filling out this questionnaire, as it usually takes place on their last day, after they have already received their final paycheck. Why wouldn't they share their thoughts and feelings with you? They have nothing to lose, and the company has everything to gain from their input.

Use both written and oral communications to get the facts and the flavor of what's behind an employee's decision to leave.

As a result of our exit questionnaires and interviews, we've:

- Provided flex-time schedules.
- Added management-training programs to improve supervision skills.
- Revamped our compensation packages.
- Initiated an incentive plan for departments not already participating in pay-for-performance programs.
- Improved the timeliness of our performance reviews.
- Developed an employee data bank.

All these things have been changes for the better.

But exit interviews have also fostered the status quo. We've learned what employees value in our workplace. Repeatedly, employees have told us the most important things to them are:

- Recognition.
- Communication with each other and with management.
- Stability of the company.
- Compensation.

The first two items, of course, can be summed up as "teamwork." They confirm for us that our management approach is on the right track.

Other exit comments help you know which managers to pat on the back. Employees who are about to become free agents have every reason to tell you the truth about how they think their coaches/managers perform.

One particular idea that came from these exit interviews really excites us: Creating an *employee data bank* at Business Interiors. We are building an employee data base that will include everyone's education, technical skills, short-term aspirations, and long-term career goals. We don't ever want to hear an exiting employee say he or she wanted to be in another department and didn't see any way to get there. Our goal is to help people find their niche. Any manager who is thinking of filling a position by going outside our company will now be instructed to check our internal data base first. If they do, they might discover that a warehouse worker, who has learned data processing at night, might be perfect for that information-processing job that has just opened up, or that we have a driver who would love to work an entry-level job in the customer-service department.

Every departing employee receives a personal letter from me thanking them for the job they did while employed by our company and also for their comments on the exit interview. I want them to know, even though they have left our employment, how much we appreciate them, and also the action we will take as a result of their comments on the exit interview.

## CONSIDER THE PARKING-LOT EXERCISE

With the emphasis on keeping good employees, the thought of terminating poor performers should create tremors. Obviously, you should do everything in your power to see that underperforming employees improve.

However, that does not mean that everyone you hire should be guaranteed lifetime employment. If you don't periodically weed out people who just can't be saved, you send the wrong message to the players who are giving you 110 percent every day.

At a seminar years ago, someone told me the secret of how one CEO ended up with all top performers.

The story goes that he assembled all his employees out on the company parking lot one morning to talk about the company's goals and objectives for the coming year. Then he started reading off a list of names.

"Those were the names of our top performers," he said, once he had finished. "They can return to work. The rest of you are dismissed. If we need you, we'll call you back within a week. If you don't hear from us, you're terminated."

I don't know whether the story is true, but I do know that companies who want to maintain an excellent staff *routinely* have to look at nonperformers and evaluate the effect they are having on company profits. After you've coached, counseled, and cajoled, you have to realize what keeping nonperformers on the team and payroll is costing you in morale and profits.

Occasionally, weeding out our poorer performers means we lose someone who means a lot to us personally. Some can't keep up with our fast growth. Some have been transferred into jobs that don't match their skills. Whatever the reason, losing an employee hurts.

But even terminating a poor performer can reinforce what's right with your company. If handled properly, the exit interview can be a positive experience for someone you're taking out of the game. Your honest evaluation of a poor performer might direct him into something he's more suited for.

He might even thank you. Two weeks after we terminated a poor performer, a new job applicant listed the terminated employee as a referral. "Howard says this is a great place to work," he told us. Two months later the same terminated employee phoned us with a sales lead!

Management has a responsibility to constantly grade employees on how well they are doing. At Business Interiors, we use a four-point scale, with 1 being the highest rating. In our system, 3 is minimally acceptable and a 4 means you aren't cutting the mustard. If you are a 4—we definitely let you know that's your rating—we will work with you to help you improve. We will coach you, to see if there are any problems we can resolve. We'll offer you additional training, and management will work with you on a one-on-one basis. However if, after all that, you still remain a 4, we'll have to let you go.

We also work with our 3s to get them to increase their ratings to at least a 2. Employees have to know how they are perceived by management. Your company's growth and profitability depend on you having the best possible people on your team.

## WATCH THOSE SUFFERING FROM ''BA''

Some people suffer from bad breath or BO. Others suffer from BA—bad attitude. Negativism.

Being around these people is like stepping into quicksand. They'll destroy the team spirit of those they work with. If you counseled them about their attitude and it doesn't change, quickly get them off the field—*permanently*. If their attitude doesn't come around, it can zap the whole team.

A positive climate and team spirit among your employees rubs off on your customers. Treat loyal employees as you treat loyal customers.

### COACH'S CHECKLIST

✓ *Conduct exit interviews.* Nobody wants to lose good employees. But if they are going to leave, conduct exit interviews—both oral and written—and pay attention to the results. If it's the employee's decision to leave, there is little reason for him or her not to tell you the truth.

✓ *Cut your losses with nonperformers.* Nobody likes to fire people, but if you keep nonperformers around, you are going to hurt the morale of the rest of your team.

✓ *Make your people proud of where they work.* If they're not proud, you can be sure that they are not doing their best, and you also can be sure that they are communicating—in some way—to your customers their feelings about your company.

# Epilogue

# The Coach's Final Checklist: Teamwork Makes It Happen!

> *Innovation creates opportunity; quality creates demand; but teamwork makes it happen!*

LET ME offer some final tips for fielding a successful corporate team.

*Scout the competition.* Find out what your customers want, and what the competition is not supplying, then add those missing products and services to your line. It sounds simple, but can you say with absolute certainty that you know every single place where your competition is vulnerable? Scout the competition.

And as long as you are scouting, scout yourself as well. Determine what internal problems you have that are keeping your team from doing its best. You might have managers who are not sharing information that their team needs, because they are afraid of losing control. Other managers may be suffering from NIH, the "not-invented-here" syndrome.

And be sure to scout your employees. You can be certain that your competition is.

Do your employees say things like:

"Not another meeting—I don't have the time to waste."

"Groups just maintain the mediocre."

"I don't want to hassle people or have them hassle me about performance or decisions."

"We won't have any real authority anyway."

"What's in it for me?"

"That's not my job."

Find out what you are up against—both internally and externally—before you start to play.

*Create a bottom-up strategy.* Make sure all your executives believe in the team concept. In addition, they need to be totally committed to customer service and quality, and they must also agree to totally open communication throughout your company—upward, downward, laterally.

What this really means is that they must focus on goal-setting, allow risk-taking, and provide resources and time. It means they'll cut red tape—throw away the need for four levels of approval signatures—and give front-line people and teams power to implement their ideas. It means they'll train people so they'll know how to act in groups, lead meetings, communicate, listen, plan, and handle conflict. Perhaps most of all, it means that they'll reward teamwork.

Only after you've laid this groundwork can you divide all departments into teams and coach them to compete individually against their past records/quotas/standards/norms, and also have them compete as a group against other teams in your company, and against industry groups and industry norms.

Once you divide your departments into teams, take the next step. Set up teams that cross departmental lines so that you can address issues of quality, customer service, innovation, and other organizational goals such as the creation of an internal environment that makes it fun to go to work in the morning.

Invite all your teams to strategy sessions where you identify and discuss your *WOTS*—weaknesses, opportunities, threats, and strengths—and *Wishes*—the things they'd love to have. Then provide opportunities for them to implement their own ideas. Let others, both inside and outside their department, offer coaching help.

Finally, get started. Mike Miller frequently reminds himself of something that General George S. Patton once said: "A good plan violently executed today is better than the perfect plan executed tomorrow."

*Select quarterbacks who can handle a huddle.* As the NFL proves almost every Sunday, you can't depend on one quarterback for the whole season. They have bad days. They get hurt. They demand to be traded.

Similarly, you can't have your company rely on just one leader. You need to make a constant effort to develop bench strength, people who can step up and assume a leadership role as the need arises.

Here's what we look for in potential managers:

**L** Listening. They listen with an open mind to other players and coaches.

**E** Empowering viewpoint. They delegate and enable others to act.

**A** Ambition. They have goals, imagination, and vision.

**D** Desire. They show enthusiasm, drive, and determination.

**E** Example. They serve as a role model for the ideals they believe in: honesty, common sense, and hard work.

**R** Respect. Leaders respect individuals and build self-esteem.

**S** Self-esteem. They show poise, and believe in themselves so they don't "have something to prove" to others.

**H** Heart. They empathize and encourage.

**I** Initiative. They have the energy to make things happen.

**P** Patience. They are slow to criticize, quick to praise.

Coaching, which is an act of leadership, has to be learned. It's a process. It's not something that comes out of a box.

And just as with customer service, leaders have "moments of truth" with their teams. Do they ask the right question at the right time to investigate, gain feedback, analyze, and set the course? Will they build stress and create tension? Will they challenge the team to achieve? Will they "pull rank"?

Some people have worked all their life to get the title "boss." Are they now willing to share their power? Will they really share information? Are they willing to take the risks that come with letting their team make decisions on their own? Will they blame people when things don't work?

Will players feel comfortable with them? Are the coaches organized? Will they follow through on the details? Can they run interference, if need be, and gain cooperation with other teams on joint projects or problems?

Just like your employees, leaders—coaches—need to be trained.

*Make sure the passer and receiver can play together.* To create team spirit, team members must learn to trust one another. Players must believe in their teammates—their ethics, their reliability, their sincerity, their goodwill, and their skill. Players have to learn to be open, straightforward, decisive, and assertive with one another.

Teams must learn to value individual players for their competence and contributions rather than just their organizational title.

And just as you can't have a team of all tackles or tailbacks, you can't have a team made up of all extroverts, all introverts, all innovators, or all rule-keepers. Accept diversity in skills and personality. You have to, if you want to develop confidence and camaraderie among your team.

Assure all team players that there's something in it for them. Make it clear that their performance will be reviewed with their team-playing skills in mind. And tie their paycheck to their participation on teams. Build in team incentives and team bonuses into your compensation plans.

Be careful, however, that the people you work with don't perceive "team players" as those who don't rock the boat, who don't question, who don't step out of line. If that's how you define team player, your team will quickly settle into mediocrity.

*Schedule practice sessions for the players.* You have to provide formal and informal training opportunities for teams: brainstorming and goal-setting sessions; workshops on problem solving and customer service.

In addition, you are going to have to work on your employee's interpersonal skills.

Some players will have to learn how to take risks.

Some will need to learn to ask questions rather than make statements; others will need to learn to make statements rather than just ask questions.

Some will need to learn to ask others for help; others will need to learn to give it.

Some will have to learn to quit telling everybody what to do; others will have to learn to quit asking somebody what to do.

Some will have to learn to think before they act; others will have to learn to act decisively.

Some will need to learn to look at the clock; others will have to train themselves not to.

Some might need confidence to speak up, and others might need the sensitivity to let them.

Everybody will have to learn flexibility and how to negotiate. Everyone will need to find a balance between their cooperative and competitive natures.

Team players will also have to be comfortable in playing other positions. Cross-training should become the rule. Customer-service people should learn what the purchasing department does, and the reverse should be true as well. Not only does this make your organization more flexible, it will reduce friction. If you truly know how hard someone else's job is, you are less likely to give them a hard time when they don't perform up to what might have been unrealistic expectations.

These practice sessions—training, conducted by outside experts if you need them—are not an interruption of work; they are a vitally important part of team work.

There are two other points to make about this. You'll have to provide opportunities for your players to spend time together in a relaxed setting so that they can understand what their teammates need in terms of personal satisfaction and emotional support. Finally, your players have to believe in results. They'll have to assume responsibility and help create a winning team.

*Plan for the kickoff.* Don't try to put the team concept into practice until you have the game plan worked out. Understand what the culture change will mean to your company. Talk with other companies who have teams in place; read; attend seminars. As a group, consider and discuss the relationships of your team. Select program champions to make things happen; these will be the people who actually go out and start building teams.

Then implement the teamwork concept, and do it right away; otherwise, you run the risk of losing the game before you begin.

It's just like customer service. When you say you're going to do something, you'd better be ready to do it. Nothing is worse than making "excellent customer service" the centerpiece of a massive advertising campaign when your staff hasn't been trained to deliver it. Having had their expectations raised, underserved customers will be all the more irate.

The same goes with teamwork. Don't start the game clock, if your players aren't ready to take the field.

*Let your teams run with the ball and get out of their way.* Share your ultimate organizational goals with your teams, and then challenge them to be creative and innovative in the how-tos.

Give them a copy of the game plan that your coaching staff has developed, then ask them to develop and run their own plays to move down the field. Stay out of their way. Coaches should be on the sidelines—not on the field.

That doesn't mean you stand by silently, though. To keep the game from overwhelming them, coach them in breaking the game down into small, achievable goals: a field goal here, a touchdown there, a solid defensive stand when it's needed.

Commit yourself to giving your team and team leaders the freedom, resources, and accountability to win.

Coach the coaches. Teach your managers how to react when a team project or decision fails. Show them the leverage that comes with delegating.

*Work the clubhouse.* Be accessible as a coach and find ways to build team spirit and camaraderie. Provide ways for your players to get to know each other on and off the field. Encourage them to give of themselves and "become family."

*Celebrate wins together.* Share your statistics. Tell the team how it's doing. Odds are they will be doing quite well.

Researchers at the American Society for Training and Development surveyed a cross-section of the Fortune 500, and the nation's biggest privately held companies, to see if they use self-directed work teams, and if they did, to see how well they worked.

Surprisingly, about a third of the companies that responded said they employed the teamwork concept, at least to some degree, and they were very pleased with the results. They reported improved productivity, job satisfaction, and customer service.

Wherever you place your goal line, let your teams measure their contributions and then celebrate their wins. Big wins, *and* small wins.

Celebrate both with rewards and recognition, and increased responsibilities and authority. Coach employees to picture themselves as a team and to celebrate their wins as a team.

Give credit where it's due, and share the spotlight of success with the whole team. Team success and individual success are synonymous.

There is no question: *Teamwork makes it happen!*"

# INDEX

# To Contact Jim Miller

Jim Miller can be reached for keynote speeches, seminars, and motivational presentations through:

> **JIM MILLER ENTERPRISES**
> P.O. Box 200997
> Arlington, Texas 76006-0997
> (817) 640-2403

Popular current presentation titles include:

- *Road Map for Success*

- *How to Feel Like a Million Without Spending a Nickel!*

- *Corporate Coaching*

- *How to Profit Through Service and Teamwork*

- *How to Thrive and Survive in a Family Business*

- *Providing Sales Leadership for Your Growth*

New programs constantly are being introduced in order to respond to changes in workplace conditions and industry needs. Jim Miller customizes his presentations to each client's needs.

There are few speakers who have the enthusiasm and electric spark to motivate a group as Jim Miller does. He keeps his audiences both entertained and totally involved, and he always leaves them with positive formulas that they can successfully use on a daily basis in both their business and their personal lives. Participants in Jim's seminars often have said, "Hearing Jim Miller was like getting a blood transfusion."